Management As
MISSION

JOHN OBERG, DSW, MBA
KRISTIAN JALOWAY, MPHIL, MPIA

Preface

Parish leadership is one of the most rewarding and challenging roles in the Church. While pastors are called to guide their communities spiritually, they also bear the responsibility of governance, which includes managing the many facets of parish life—organizing resources, leading staff and volunteers, and ensuring that everything aligns with the mission of evangelization. The reality is that these tasks require not only a deep spiritual commitment but also practical skills in management and leadership.

That's why we've written this book. We understand that for many pastors, the management side of parish life can feel overwhelming, especially when they are also deeply focused on their community's spiritual and pastoral needs. Our goal is to provide a guide that blends spiritual leadership with effective management, thereby creating a holistic approach that supports the Church's mission.

The principles that guide us come from the Word of God, expressed in Scripture and Tradition, magisterial documents, and of course the many examples of saints and innovators in the history of the Church. In this way we can stay faithful to the core of our faith, that can never change, while having the confidence and courage to be open to growth and progress when it comes to the things that can and should change over time as the people and environment we operate in change.

As advisors, we've spent years working with parishes across the country, helping them to implement management systems that foster alignment, accountability, and growth.

At John Oberg Advisory, we've had the privilege of partnering with countless parishes, offering guidance and support as they navigate the complexities of operations and the difficulties of a radically different environment. Over the years, we've developed a vast toolkit designed specifically for the Church's unique needs. This toolkit includes practical strategies, templates, and systems to help parishes run smoothly while staying mission-focused. Above all, we focus on teaching the knowledge and skills necessary to use these tools effectively.

This book is intended to be an overview and introduction to that larger toolkit. It provides the foundational principles and strategies that will help any parish leader get started on the path to more effective leadership and management. We've distilled years of experience and practical insights into these chapters, offering clear, actionable steps that can immediately benefit your parish.

However, this book is just the beginning. Our system goes far deeper, addressing everything from detailed financial management to long-term strategic planning, staff development, and parishioner engagement and growth. As you work through the concepts presented here, know that you are engaging with the first layer of a comprehensive approach to parish management.

Our mission at John Oberg Advisory is to help pastors and parish leaders not only manage their parishes effectively but to also thrive in their roles, balancing pastoral care with administrative excellence. We believe that when parishes are well-managed, they can better fulfill their spiritual mission. Through this book—and through our tools and support—we hope to equip you with the skills and confidence needed to lead your parish with clarity, grace, and purpose.

We are excited to share this journey with you and look forward to seeing how these principles transform your parish into a thriving, mission-driven community, no matter where you find yourself currently.

Table of
Contents

01
CHAPTER

> "And whatever you do, in word or in deed, do everything in the name of the Lord Jesus, giving thanks to God the Father through him."

COLOSSIANS 3:17 (NABRE)

Management as Mission

In the heart of every Catholic parish lies a mission field often overlooked—the business office. This book aims to shed light on the incredible potential of transforming parish management into a vibrant center of evangelization and discipleship. By aligning our day-to-day practices with our spiritual goals, we can breathe new life into our communities and reignite the flame of faith in the hearts of our parishioners.

Throughout time, and true today, the world hungers for leadership. At times, society has looked to the Church as a leader beyond the spiritual journey, which has created moments ripe for evangelization or discipleship. In retrospect, this has been true in education, healthcare, and industry. There have also been times when people have perceived the Church less in these areas. This book offers a way that we can improve the Church's administration as a byproduct of our divine calling. We don't administer to be worldly but instead meet the world to draw people to the faith and to help them deepen their faith.

The Catholic Church's history is a rich tapestry woven with threads of triumph and challenge, a testament to the enduring power of faith in the face of an ever-changing world. To understand where we stand today, let's take a quick journey through the Church's role as a leader and light in society.

From the apostolic age, when Christianity spread like wildfire through the authentic joy and charity of its followers, to the era of Christendom, our faith has always adapted to the times. In those early days, the Church was a grassroots movement, fueled by the passion of ordinary people who encountered Christ's transformative love. Their radiant lives, marked by selfless sacrifice, drew others to the faith in droves, despite being persecuted by the Roman Empire.

As Christianity's influence grew, so did its impact on the world. The Church became a pioneer in various fields, shaping society in profound ways. In healthcare, it established some of the first hospitals during the Middle Ages. The Hospital of St. John in Jerusalem, founded in the eleventh century, was one of the earliest examples of a hospital, providing care for all, regardless of faith. These institutions laid the foundation for modern healthcare systems, emphasizing compassion, charity, and the value of human life.

The Church's impact on education was equally significant. It founded some of the first universities in Europe, like the Universities of Paris and Oxford, which became

centers for the study of theology, arts, law, and medicine. This commitment to learning fostered a culture of intellectual curiosity and critical thinking that continues to shape our educational institutions.

In the economic sphere, the Church played a crucial role in developing early banking practices. The Knights Templar established one of the first forms of banking to aid pilgrims. The Church's teachings influenced ethical economic practices, emphasizing concepts like fair trade and just prices. These principles laid the groundwork for more equitable and sustainable economic systems.

The Church's involvement in trade and commerce was evident in medieval markets and fairs often held on church grounds. Religious orders like the Benedictines and Cistercians promoted international trade, facilitating the exchange of goods, ideas, and cultural practices across Europe.

Financial innovations, such as the development of credit systems, can also be traced back to the Church. The concept of *montes pietatis*, charitable pawnbrokers set up by Franciscans, were precursors to modern banking. The Church's need to transfer large sums of money led to the early use of bills of exchange, playing a crucial role in the development of modern banking.

The Church's teachings shaped ethical business practices, influencing laws against usury and developing concepts like the "just price." In more recent times, it has been a strong advocate for labor rights and social justice, consistently fighting for workers' rights, fair wages, and humane working conditions.

Yet, despite shaping Western society, as centuries passed, the ground beneath the Church's feet began to shift once more. Today, we find ourselves in a new apostolic age, where more than half the population claims no religious affiliation. The traditional methods of parish life, with their emphasis on large events and high volume of sacraments, no longer seem to resonate with a world yearning for authentic connection and transformative spirituality.

For many newly appointed pastors, and even seasoned ones, this shifting landscape presents a daunting challenge. Trained in theology and pastoral care, they find themselves at the helm of what is essentially a small business, grappling with finance, human resources, and administrative management. The weight of these responsibilities can be overwhelming, pulling them away from their true calling as shepherds of souls.

But amidst this chaos, there is hope. By embracing a new perspective that sees parish management not as a burden but as an opportunity for mission, we can align every aspect of parish life with the goal of evangelization and discipleship. Through a systematic approach that draws on biblical principles of leadership, we can transform our administrative operations into centers of grace and growth.

This transformation begins with a willingness to learn, to step outside the comfort zone of traditional parish management, and explore innovative ways of thinking and acting. It requires deep trust in the Holy Spirit's guidance and a commitment to ongoing formation for every member of the parish staff.

We'll explore practical strategies for aligning our parish management with our spiritual mission. We'll help you understand how to manage the processes of budgeting, human resources, facilities maintenance, and more, always keeping discipleship at the forefront. By approaching these tasks with a missionary mindset, we can transform even the most mundane aspects of parish administration into opportunities for grace and encounter.

As we embark on this journey, let's draw strength from the Church's long history of leadership and service. Let's remember that our work in the parish office is not just a job but a calling—a participation in the ongoing mission of the Church to bring Christ's love and truth to the world. With faith, creativity, and perseverance, we can build parishes that are not just surviving but thriving—beacons of hope and transformation in a world that desperately needs the light of the Gospel.

The Challenges of Modern Parish Management

Before we get to solutions too quickly, let's talk a little more about the challenges and the root causes. In recent years, the Catholic Church has found itself grappling with a new set of challenges, particularly in the realm of parish management. As society has grown increasingly complex and fast-paced, the demands placed on pastors have multiplied, leaving many feeling overwhelmed and ill-equipped to navigate the intricacies of running a parish.

One of the most significant challenges facing pastors today is the sheer volume of administrative tasks that fall under their purview. From managing finances and facilities to overseeing staff and volunteers, the role of a pastor has expanded far

beyond the traditional duties of preaching, teaching, and pastoral care. For many, this shift has been a source of great stress and anxiety, as they struggle to balance the spiritual needs of their flock with the practical demands of running a parish

Priests reading this already know it, but let us illustrate the point with a story from one of our clients. Fr. Sam had a deep conversion experience during his college years and eventually went through RCIA and was received into the Catholic Church. His experience in a vibrant campus ministry environment was beautiful and he loved his newfound faith and community. He is excited to share his faith, and through that experience feels the call to do it for his whole life as a priest. After the additional 7 years he is finally ordained and receives his first pastoral assignment. He spends 3 years serving as a parochial vicar, making a difference in so many hearts and lives. Now he gets his first assignment as pastor, and he feels he is truly the spiritual father to these souls. The first day in the office a staff member asks to speak with him and reveals that there is a lot of internal conflict, people are ready to leave their jobs, and if he doesn't do something quickly she might leave too. Day two he is preparing his homily and gets a call that a pipe burst in the sacristy and he spends the rest of the day helping clean up and trying to find a reasonably priced plumber to come fix it. Day three he is able to say his first Sunday Masses as pastor. He loves meeting so many young families. After one Mass an elderly gentleman comes up and says, hey father, I'm glad you're here, but I do want to say that we need you to preach more about the political situation in the country and, without mincing words too much, says that if he doesn't many of the more generous donors like himself will be moving parishes. The main Mass has a nice choir but he notices the music at the other Masses is pretty pathetic. He's not sure he should take a day off on Monday, with all these problems going on, but he takes half a day then comes back to check on the plumbing repairs. After a month, Fr. Sam is really questioning whether he is suited to be a pastor. His life is now one of meetings, problems, and much less time for pastoral ministry. He wonders how long he can keep up this pace as he is already noticing he's gaining weight from not having time to exercise and eating mostly fast food, since he doesn't have much time to cook anything.

Compounding this challenge is the fact that many pastors, like Fr. Sam, enter their roles with little to no formal training in business or management. Seminary education, while invaluable in preparing priests for the spiritual and theological aspects of their vocation, often falls short when it comes to equipping them with the practical skills needed to lead a parish effectively. Priests are being assigned as pastors after just a few years of priestly experience. As a result, many pastors find themselves learning on the job, a process that can be both time-consuming and fraught with trial and error.

The consequences of this lack of preparation can be severe. Pastors who are overwhelmed by the demands of parish management may find themselves neglecting their primary duties of teaching and sanctifying. They may struggle to build and maintain healthy relationships with their staff and volunteers, leading to high turnover rates and a lack of continuity in parish programs and ministries. They may also find themselves, or others around them, making costly mistakes in areas such as finance and human resources, putting the long-term stability of the parish at risk. Although thankfully not the norm, there are high rates of financial fraud in the Church due to lack of good accounting practices and oversight. On the other hand, some in pastoral care neglect administrative duties altogether. Without a balance between caring for their flock and keeping the nuts and bolts of their parish up and running, a church may very well find itself having to close its doors.

Perhaps most disturbingly, the stress and burnout that can result from these challenges can take a profound toll on the mental and physical health of pastors themselves. Studies have shown that clergy are at a higher risk for depression, anxiety, and other mental health issues than the general population, a reality that has only been exacerbated by the demands of modern parish life.[1]

Many hear these issues and are quick to ask why seminary formation doesn't solve these problems. While it is a valid question, our experience in education, as well as many conversations with both priests, bishops and seminary formators, lead us to believe that changing seminary formation won't fix these issues completely. The U.S. Bishops are constantly looking at these issues and have recently issued a revised Plan of Priestly Formation, or PPF, with a new Propaedeutic year, as well as a year right before priestly ordination. We believe this is encouraging, but it will not solve the problem of lack of organizational skills. There is little space in the curriculum for business training, and knowledge alone cannot create the leadership skills needed to be effective in today's world. Also, when a pastor faces a specific issue like an employee who shows up to a meeting clearly drunk, he is unlikely to call his seminary professor to walk him through the necessary steps to take. Nor is his professor probably available in a timely manner to accompany all of his former students in their current crisis.

----

1   {https://www.ncbi.nlm.nih.gov/pmc/articles/PMC8364777/}

Another logical solution is mentorship. We wholeheartedly agree that mentoring is a helpful tool, and there are some more experienced pastors who make excellent mentors, although others do not have the knowledge nor skills needed to mentor well. The biggest challenge with mentoring by itself is that it does little to address the need for innovation when a new mindset is needed. Indeed, some priests went through seminary formation years before, in a solidly Christendom mindset, sometimes with little emphasis on personal spiritual growth, and are unlikely to be able to think outside the box and find innovative solutions from other areas that have already solved these kinds of problems. Other mentors might be from the business world, the military, nonprofit ministries, and so forth. The biggest challenge with those relationships tend to be that they speak a different language than our priests do. So finding a good mentor is a challenge, but it does help to provide someone to discuss issues with and learn from the wisdom of our elders.

What can substantially improve the possibility of these types of approaches? Leadership needs to make a significant difference by having a clear, overarching framework that provides a system with vocabulary and concepts that everyone can work on together.

In light of these challenges, it is clear that a new approach to parish management is needed, one that recognizes the unique role of the pastor as a holistic leader who meets people in the world through the lens of eternal fruit. This approach must be grounded in a deep understanding of the mission of the Church and a commitment to aligning every aspect of parish life with that mission.

At its core, this new approach must begin with a recognition of the inherent dignity and value of every person involved in the life of the parish, from the pastor and staff to the volunteers and parishioners. It must prioritize the formation and empowerment of lay leaders in canonically appropriate roles, recognizing that the work of evangelization and discipleship is not the responsibility of the pastor alone but rather the shared calling of every baptized Christian. A disorganized apostolic effort will generally lead to mediocre results. St. Paul speaks of putting on the whole armor of God in Ephesians 6:10-18. What does this mean in the context of calling forth every member of the Church to work together to promote not only the Gospel but to glorify God? This is spiritual warfare, and we are called to actively live out our faith in the world. As St. James says, "Faith without works is dead." Can God take our mediocrity and make miracles? Yes, of course, but should we expect miracles to do the work for us when we have tools in front of us to help us get organized and produce a better vineyard? Our answer is really both/and. We need to be as organized as we can with the tools we have, knowing that it is always God who produces the fruit on the vine. (John 15:5)

Furthermore, this approach must be marked by a spirit of collaboration and teamwork, one that values the unique gifts and talents of every member of the parish community. It must foster a culture of transparency and accountability, where decisions are made in the light of the Gospel and the teachings of the Church, and where every person is held to the highest standards of integrity and professionalism. In a wayward world, where people nowadays value "living their own truth," it is more vital than ever to share God's Truth. People are seeking meaning in their lives and will look to fill that void. Many are looking elsewhere. The Church needs to reignite its passion in speaking Truth, as people can only find true freedom when it's found in Christ. Otherwise, we are slaves to our sin. At the same time, we need to do this in the most charitable way, because people will generally only listen when they know we love them.

Finally, this approach must be anchored in a deep trust in the guidance and grace of the Holy Spirit. It must recognize that the work of parish management is ultimately a work of faith, one that requires a willingness to step out in courage and conviction, even in the face of uncertainty and challenge.

As we explore the practical strategies and insights needed to implement this new approach, we must keep these core principles at the forefront of our minds. For it is only by grounding our efforts in the truth of the Gospel and the wisdom of the Church that we can hope to transform our parish offices into true centers of discipleship, places where every person is welcomed, valued, and empowered to live out their baptismal calling with joy and fidelity.

Transforming the Parish Office into a Center of Evangelism and Discipleship

At the heart of this new approach to parish management lies a fundamental shift in perspective, one that sees the parish office not merely as a center of administrative tasks but rather as a vibrant hub of evangelization and discipleship. This shift requires a deep commitment to the formation and empowerment of every person involved in the life of the parish, from the pastor and staff to the volunteers and parishioners.

The first step in this process is the evangelization and discipleship of the parish staff themselves. All too often, the focus of parish formation programs is directed outward, towards the wider community, while the spiritual needs of those who serve the parish on a daily basis are overlooked. Yet, if we are to truly transform our parish offices into centers of discipleship, we must begin by investing in the faith lives of our own team members.

This investment can take many forms, from regular opportunities for prayer and reflection to ongoing training and professional development. It may involve the creation of small faith-sharing groups among staff members, where they can support and encourage one another in their own journeys of discipleship. It may also require a reevaluation of hiring practices, to ensure that every member of the team is not only professionally qualified but also deeply committed to the Church's mission and values.

As the parish staff grows in their own faith and sense of purpose, they become powerful agents of evangelization. Through their daily interactions with parishioners and visitors, they have the opportunity to model the joy and love of Christ in tangible ways, from the warmth of their welcome to the efficiency and professionalism of their service. In this way, the parish office becomes not just a place where business is conducted but a true reflection of God's hospitality and grace.

Of course, the transformation of the parish office into a center of discipleship extends beyond the staff. It requires a renewed commitment to the formation and empowerment of lay leaders, recognizing that every baptized Christian is called to share in the mission of the Church. This may involve the creation of new leadership roles and ministries within the parish, as well as the provision of ongoing training and support for those who serve in these roles.

One powerful example of this approach can be seen in the development of small group ministries within the parish. By creating opportunities for parishioners to gather in intimate, faith-sharing communities, the parish office can foster a sense of belonging and purpose that extends far beyond the church's walls. These groups can become incubators of discipleship, places where individuals can grow in their relationship with Christ and with one another and where they can discern their unique gifts and callings in service to the wider community.

Another key aspect of transforming the parish office into a center of discipleship is the cultivation of an ethos of stewardship. This involves not only the responsible management of financial resources but also the nurturing of a spirit of generosity and sacrifice among all members of the parish community. By teaching and modeling the principles of Christian stewardship, the parish office can help parishioners to see their time, talent, and treasure not as private possessions but as gifts to be shared in service to the Church's mission .

Ultimately, the transformation of the parish office into a center of discipleship requires a profound trust in the power and guidance of the Holy Spirit. Parishioners and leaders alike must be in prayer for discernment and direction. It demands a willingness to let go of old ways of thinking and acting and to embrace new possibilities for growth and renewal. It calls for a spirit of creativity and innovation, one that is always seeking new ways to proclaim the Gospel and invite others into a life-changing relationship with Jesus Christ.

As we continue to explore the practical strategies and insights needed to bring about this transformation, let us keep our eyes fixed on the ultimate goal: the building up of the Body of Christ, one disciple at a time. For it is in the faithful witness of our parish offices, and in the lives of those who serve and are served by them, that the world will come to know God's love and mercy.

Aligning Parish Resources for Mission

As we seek to transform our parish offices into centers of discipleship, it is essential that we also take a hard look at the way we steward the resources entrusted to our care. Every parish, no matter its size or location, has been blessed with a unique combination of human, financial, and material resources, all of which are intended to support the mission of evangelization and discipleship.

Yet, all too often, these resources are not aligned with the mission in a way that maximizes their impact. Funds may be allocated to programs or initiatives that do not directly support the work of evangelization, while talented staff members and volunteers may find themselves in roles that do not fully utilize their gifts and passions. The result is a parish that is not operating at its complete potential, a community that is not fully living out its call to be a light to the world.

The process of aligning parish resources for mission begins with a clear understanding of the parish's unique identity and purpose. This requires prayerful discernment on

the part of the pastor and leadership team, as well as input from the wider parish community. It may involve the development of a mission statement or pastoral plan that articulates the specific ways in which the parish seeks to proclaim the Gospel and make disciples in its particular context.

With this clarity of purpose in place, the next step is to conduct a thorough assessment of the parish's current resources. This may involve a review of financial statements and budgets, as well as an inventory of the skills and talents of staff members and volunteers. It may also require an evaluation of the parish's physical assets, such as buildings and equipment, to determine how they can be best utilized in service to the mission.

Based on this assessment, the parish leadership team can make strategic decisions about the allocation of resources. This may involve a reallocation of funds towards programs or initiatives that directly support evangelization and discipleship, such as youth ministry, adult faith formation, or outreach to the poor and marginalized. It may also require a reorganization of staff roles and responsibilities, to ensure that every team member is working in a way that maximizes their gifts and talents.

One key aspect of aligning parish resources for mission is the development of a culture of collaboration and teamwork. This involves breaking down silos between different ministries and departments, fostering a sense of shared responsibility for the work of evangelization. It may require the creation of cross-functional teams or working groups, where staff members and volunteers from different areas of the parish come together to plan and execute key initiatives.

Another important factor in aligning parish resources for mission is the cultivation of a spirit of innovation and creativity. This involves a willingness to take risks and try new approaches, even if they involve a departure from the way things have always been done. It may require a shift in mindset from a maintenance mentality, focused on preserving the status quo, to a mission mentality, focused on continual growth and adaptation to changing circumstances

Ultimately, the alignment of parish resources for mission is an ongoing process of discernment and adaptation. It requires a commitment to regular evaluation and assessment, to ensure that the parish remains focused on its core purpose and is making the most effective use of its resources. It also requires a spirit of openness and flexibility, a willingness to pivot and adjust course as needed in response to changing needs and opportunities.

As we seek to align our parish resources for mission, let us keep in mind the words of St. Paul: "And whatever you do, in word or deed, do everything in the name of the Lord Jesus, giving thanks to God the Father through him" (Colossians 3:17). May every decision we make, every resource we steward, be guided by a deep desire to serve Christ and his Church, and to lead others into the fullness of life and love that he alone can offer.

Embracing a Systematic Approach to Parish Management

As we work to transform our parish offices into centers of discipleship and align our resources for mission, it is essential that we also embrace a systematic approach to parish management. This involves the development of clear processes, policies, and procedures that ensure the smooth and effective operation of the parish, while also freeing up the pastor and leadership team to focus on the essential work of evangelization.

Before delving further into this subject, let us remember the importance of consulting the Scriptures for guidance. The New Testament is rife with directions on how to lead and conduct the Church. Everyone possesses different spiritual gifts that ought to be used to glorify God and produce fruits of the Spirit, after all.

One key aspect of a systematic approach to parish management is the creation of a clear organizational structure. This involves defining roles and responsibilities for every member of the parish staff, as well as establishing clear lines of communication and accountability. It may require the development of job descriptions and performance evaluations, as well as regular opportunities for feedback and professional development.

Another important element of a systematic approach is the establishment of standardized processes for key areas of parish life, such as sacramental preparation, liturgical planning, and financial management. This involves the creation of written policies and procedures that ensure consistency and continuity, even in the face of staff turnover or other transitions. It may also require the use of technology and software tools to streamline processes and improve efficiency.

A systematic approach to parish management also involves the regular gathering and analysis of data. This may include tracking attendance at Mass and other parish events, as well as gathering feedback from parishioners through surveys and other means. By regularly measuring key metrics and indicators, the parish leadership team can gain valuable insights into the health and vitality of the community, and make data-driven decisions about where to focus resources and attention.

Of course, embracing a systematic approach to parish management is not without its challenges. It requires a significant investment of time and resources upfront, as well as a willingness to change long-standing habits and ways of doing things. It may also require a shift in mindset, from a reactive, crisis-driven mode of operation to a proactive, strategic one.

However, the benefits of a systematic approach are well worth the effort. By creating clear structures and processes, the parish can operate with greater efficiency and effectiveness, freeing up time and energy for the essential work of evangelization. By gathering and analyzing data, the leadership team can make informed decisions and respond more nimbly to changing needs and circumstances. And by involving the whole parish community in the process, the parish can foster a greater sense of ownership and investment in the mission.

Ultimately, the goal of a systematic approach to parish management is not to create a rigid, bureaucratic structure but rather to create a framework that supports and sustains the work of discipleship. It is about creating a culture of excellence and accountability, where every member of the parish community is empowered to use their gifts and talents in service to the mission. You need as much structure as necessary to be well organized and effective, while keeping it as light as possible for your size of parish, diocese, or ministry.

As we seek to embrace a systematic approach to parish management, let us keep in mind the words of St. Paul: "All things must be done properly and in order" (1 Corinthians 14:40). May our efforts to create order and structure in our parish life always be guided by a deep love for Christ and his Church, and a desire to create a community that radiates his love and mercy to the world.

Embracing Management as Mission

We have explored the challenges and opportunities facing pastors and parish leaders in the modern world. We have seen how the demands of parish management can often feel overwhelming, pulling us away from our primary calling to be shepherds of souls. Yet, we have also discovered that by embracing management as mission, we can transform our parish offices into true centers of evangelization and discipleship, where every person is met where they are, valued, empowered, and equipped to live out their baptismal calling.

Of course, the journey of transforming our parishes is not an easy one. It requires a deep commitment to ongoing formation and growth, a willingness to take risks and try new approaches, and a spirit of humility and openness to the guidance of the Holy Spirit. It demands that we let go of our own agendas and preferences and seek always to discern and follow the will of God for our communities. It demands discipline that focuses on the eternal returns on investment rather than worldly returns.

Yet, the rewards of this journey are beyond measure. As we work to build up the Body of Christ in our parishes, we will see lives transformed by the power of the Gospel. We will witness the joy and peace that comes from living in right relationship with God and one another. And we will experience the profound satisfaction of knowing that we have been faithful stewards of the gifts and talents entrusted to our care.

Let us embrace this call to management as mission with courage and conviction. Let us seek out the wisdom and guidance of those who have gone before us and surround ourselves with a community of support and encouragement. We should never lose sight of the goal of our efforts - the building up of the Kingdom of God, one disciple at a time.

> "*Christ has no body now but yours. No hands, no feet on earth but yours. Yours are the eyes through which he looks compassion on this world. Yours are the feet with which he walks to do good. Yours are the hands through which he blesses all the world. Yours are the hands, yours are the feet, yours are the eyes, you are his body. Christ has no body now on earth but yours.*"
>
> **ST. TERESA OF AVILA**

"

"And he gave some as apostles, others as prophets, others as evangelists, others as pastors and teachers, to equip the holy ones for the work of ministry, for building up the body of Christ, until we all attain to the unity of faith and knowledge of the Son of God, to mature manhood, to the extent of the full stature of Christ."

- - - -

EPHESIANS 4:11-13

Business Office as a Mission Field

Imagine a young man who has just completed medical school and residency. He is excited to finally be out of school and ready to heal people full-time. He practices in a small hospital for just a year and is then assigned as CEO of a medium-sized hospital in a suburb not far from where he grew up and is told the outgoing CEO will leave the keys with the secretary for him to pick up. He walks in on day one knowing almost nothing at all about the history of this hospital, the current finances, the staffing, the buildings, the underlying issues with the hospital owners, the scandals caused by past doctors, the board, or the nurses, much less the patients and their health issues. As you can imagine, it would be a daunting task and would take him several years of trial and error to understand how to run this hospital efficiently, much less make it grow and thrive. This is actually pretty similar to what many new pastors experience. Picture a young, enthusiastic priest, Fr. Joseph, who is fresh out of seminary and eager to make a difference in his new parish. He envisioned himself as a shepherd, guiding his flock closer to Christ through prayerful liturgies and well- received sacraments. However, as he steps into his role as a newly appointed pastor, he quickly finds himself confronted with a reality he hadn't anticipated - the daunting task of managing a parish, much like a business owner or CEO, but without any specific or formal training.

Fr. Joseph's story is not an isolated case. In fact, it echoes the experiences of many priests who find themselves grappling with the delicate balance between their pastoral duties and the administrative demands of running a parish. Many of them, like Fr. Joseph, come to this role with a deep love for Christ and a burning desire to serve but soon discover that the day-to-day challenges of financial management, staff oversight, and the myriad of other tasks that fall under their purview can be overwhelming.

But what if we could transform this challenge into an opportunity? What if the business office, often seen as a necessary evil, could become a vibrant center of discipleship and mission? This is the promise and the potential that lies before us. Unfortunately, the parish business office, which is an extension of the pastor and should serve his mission directly, is often irrelevant in the eyes of the average parishioner or sometimes even an obstacle. If the pastor's closest collaborators are unknown, irrelevant, or on occasion even hurtful to the average parishioner, how can parishes maintain their organizational health, much less get to the mission? This is what we help pastors and parishes do. This is why this book exists. Getting organized and healthy are important, and the majority of parish offices we know are not very well organized and, even if they want to get to the mission, don't have the ability.

We will explore how to make this vision a reality by examining the current state of alignment in parishes across the country, delve into the parish's mission within the larger context of the Church, discuss why it is important for all parishes to share a single system that is flexible, modular, and extensible to any context, and provide an overview of the system that can help us achieve our goals.

> *"The parish is not an outdated institution; precisely because it possesses great flexibility, it can assume quite different contours depending on the openness and missionary creativity of the pastor and the community."*
>
> **FRANCIS, EVANGELII GAUDIUM, §28**

Aligned Management Throughout the Church

Many church leaders would not label the challenges in the business office as the most critical, even though they may acknowledge challenges in administration. This issue is not limited to individual parishes but extends to the diocesan level as well. Diocesan leaders often observe a lack of good and consistent administrative practices, which leads to inefficiencies, wasted resources, and a diminished capacity to effectively carry out the Church's mission.

One contributing factor is the high turnover rate among pastors. According to a study by the Center for Applied Research in the Apostolate (CARA), the average length of a pastorate in the United States is a mere 6.3 years. This frequent change in leadership often leads to a complete overhaul of systems and processes with each new pastor, leaving parish staff and volunteers struggling to adapt and maintain continuity. The average business or nonprofit startup takes 8.5 years to succeed. The challenge isn't the timing; it's the restart of all systems without an underlying business operating system that everyone understands.

The cost of this constant change is significant. Lay people who have experienced multiple pastoral transitions in a short period often report feelings of frustration and disconnection. They invest time and energy into learning and adapting to new systems, only to have them uprooted when a new pastor arrives. This not only leads

to inconsistent work and poor results but also erodes the sense of community and shared purpose that is so vital to a thriving parish.

While the principle of subsidiarity rightly emphasizes the importance of local decision-making and adaptability, the lack of a cohesive framework across parishes can hinder the Church's overall effectiveness. Parishes are not meant to operate as isolated entities but rather as interconnected parts of a larger whole, working together to advance the mission of the Church.

By recognizing the importance of alignment and consistency, and by providing pastors with the tools and support they need to effectively lead their parishes, we can bridge the gaps and create a more cohesive, mission-driven Church.

What do we mean when we refer to the "business office" of the parish? We realize that some people might dislike using the word "business" at all when it comes to faith-based endeavors due to their experiences with unethical business practices. While we understand this negative connotation, when we say "business office," we are referring to the place and all the work that is an extension of the pastor's work outside of the Sacraments themselves. Sometimes it is just referred to as the parish office, staffed by volunteers, paid employees, or both. The office is a place where we do our work and service. It is distinct and different from the place we pray and celebrate the liturgy, but of course, it should support and often coordinate the liturgical and sacramental life of the Church.

The sacraments are a wonderful model for alignment in the Church. Receiving the Eucharist is fundamentally a global experience. While the Rites are highly prescribed, many elements are left up to the bishops to decide, and others are up to the individual celebrant. Similarly, a greater degree of fundamental consistency throughout the work of the Church would allow us to deliberately build more loving, fruitful communities. It would allow us to minimize the time, talent, and energy we spend on matters that do not support, and sometimes actively hurt, the evangelization and discipleship we seek. This book outlines the fundamentals that are necessary as we further the Kingdom of Heaven on Earth.

As we move forward, let us keep in mind the words of St. Paul in his letter to the Ephesians: "And he gave some as apostles, others as prophets, others as evangelists, others as pastors and teachers, to equip the holy ones for the work of ministry, for building up the body of Christ, until we all attain to the unity of faith and knowledge

of the Son of God, to mature manhood, to the extent of the full stature of Christ."
(Ephesians 4:11-13)

Mission Of A Parish Within The Mission Of The Church

Role of the Numbers

One objection people have to talking about the "business office" is based on the belief that businesses only try to drive the "numbers". While that is sometimes true, good leaders never do that, so we want to talk a little bit about numbers here. We believe numbers are incredibly useful for our ministry, but their true value lies in helping us identify where there may be a problem—not in managing the numbers themselves or, worse, the people behind those numbers. Misapplying metrics can lead to focusing on the wrong goals and even objectifying people. We must always remember that numbers should guide our mission, not replace the heart of it.

Take the example of a person with a fever. When someone goes to the hospital with a high temperature, the medical team measures their vital signs: body temperature, heart rate, blood pressure, and oxygen levels. These numbers are crucial for diagnosing that something is wrong, but they aren't the problem in and of themselves. The fever is a symptom pointing to something deeper, such as an infection or an underlying health issue.

The medical team doesn't just focus on lowering the fever—they use the data to investigate the root cause. If they only treated the number (the fever) and not the illness behind it, the patient could remain in danger. This is a clear example of Goodhart's Law: "When a measure becomes a target, it ceases to be a good measure." In other words, if the goal becomes to reduce a number rather than using the number to understand the bigger issue, we lose sight of the true problem.

This is the key lesson: numbers should be a tool to help guide us to solutions, not the goal. Whether in healthcare, business, or ministry, the objective should always be to solve the real issue the numbers indicate, not to manipulate the numbers themselves.

Using Measurements In A Catholic Parish: Objective Data Without Objectifying People

Parishes often use metrics like Mass attendance, donations, or the number of sacraments performed each year to understand how well they are serving the community. While these numbers provide objective data, we must be careful not to objectify the people behind them.

For instance, a decline in Mass attendance might signal that something is off. But the goal shouldn't simply be to increase attendance for its own sake. Instead, we should ask deeper questions: Are parishioners feeling disconnected from the community? Do they need more meaningful liturgical experiences, better outreach, or stronger ministries? Simply increasing the numbers without understanding why people stopped coming misses the point entirely. The numbers are a tool to help guide us toward addressing the deeper needs of our parishioners.

The same applies when measuring the success of parish employees and volunteers. For example, we might evaluate a youth minister by the number of teens attending events, but that number doesn't tell the full story. What's more important is whether the youth are growing in their faith, experiencing deeper connections with God, and engaging in the life of the parish. A large number of attendees at events may look good, but if it doesn't lead to spiritual growth, the mission isn't being fulfilled.

There are some numbers that should be measured in every parish, and there are others that will depend upon the role of the parish vis-à-vis the broader church. See Chapter 3 for the different roles that parishes play, and Chapter 8 to learn about how to effectively put numbers to work objectively without objectifying people. Keep in mind that there is approximately one priest for every 20,000 lay people on the planet, and some sociologists suggest we can know 150 people deeply at a given time, so we clearly need a well-formed and organized laity if we want to span this enormous gap.

At the heart of managing a parish lies the mission to evangelize, as Christ commanded in Matthew 28:19-20: "Go therefore and make disciples of all nations." The purpose of the parish is not simply to administer the sacraments but to create a thriving community where people encounter Christ and grow as missionary disciples. While theology underpins this mission, the practical skills of management play a crucial role in achieving it. Objective data helps us measure how well we are fulfilling the mission. We must use these tools to identify areas for improvement without losing sight of the individuals and their spiritual needs. A parish is a place where the priest, through his leadership and management, evangelizes and forms both the staff and the faithful, creating a culture where spiritual growth is nurtured.

The Importance of One System and Implementing the Entire System

While having a single, simple system for every parish might bring many benefits, we've heard people object that a small rural parish and a large urban parish can't possibly both use the same system. If you understand a system as an exact model, where everything is identical, then this objection would be right. However, the operating system we propose is modular and flexible, like Lego in a way, so that each pastor can use the same system and language without being locked into a straitjacket. At the same time, implementing only certain aspects of the system while neglecting others will likely lead to suboptimal results and may even create new challenges and frustrations.

To illustrate this point, let's consider an analogy from the world of technology: the operating system of a computer. Just as a parish is a complex organism with many interconnected parts, a computer relies on a carefully designed operating system to manage its various functions and applications.

Imagine if you attempted to build your own operating system by cobbling together bits and pieces of code from different sources. Unless you were an expert in operating systems, with years of experience and a deep understanding of how all the components interact, the result would likely be a system that is unstable, inefficient, and prone to crashes. So it is with the parish operating system. Each component, from the foundational elements of faith, values, mission, and strategy, to the practical tools for administration and discipleship, is designed to work in harmony with the others.

The same principle applies to the system we're proposing for parish management. Each component, from the foundational elements of faith, values, mission, and strategy, to the practical tools for administration and discipleship, is designed to work in harmony with the others. Attempting to pick and choose only certain parts is like trying to run a computer with an incomplete or mismatched operating system.

Furthermore, implementing a cohesive system across a parish requires a significant investment of time, energy, and resources. It demands a willingness to learn new ways of thinking and working, to challenge long-held assumptions, and to step out in faith and trust. Attempting to shortcut this process by implementing only certain aspects of the system is not only ineffective but can also breed resentment and resistance among staff and volunteers, who may feel that their efforts are being wasted or undermined.

Let's share a cautionary tale about well-meaning business expertise being misapplied in a parish setting. A successful, well-meaning businessperson volunteers to help a parish facing financial and attendance challenges. With the best intentions, they implement corporate strategies that create success in their career but likely in a slightly different context than what is needed in the parish. Missing the subtle nuance can create a lot of chaos in the parish, leading many pastors to want nothing to do with anything that smells like "business."

Let's give an example to show what we mean. Perhaps that well-intentioned business person tells the pastor, "Why are our Mass attendance numbers so low? And why are most of the people in the parish elderly? If I had a business competitor who was getting more people than I was, I would see if I could implement what is working for them to get more people in the door. We need to imitate that protestant church down the road and get more modern music at Mass, and hire a better youth minister who can really bring in the kids and young people." Many Catholic churches have tried these strategies in the last decades, and they seemed to be successful judging by the number of kids in their youth groups, but they missed the subtle distinction from their sacramental theology that the goal of the Church is not to have more sacraments, because sacraments are the means to an end. The goal of the Catholic Church, and of the sacraments, is to bring people to Grace, or another way to say it is we want to give people an encounter with the saving Lord. This apparently small distinction makes all the difference in the strategy we pick as a parish.

As trusted advisors to many pastors, we've spent years developing management operating systems across several industries, are recognized as teachers of the topic at research universities, and have studied the specific needs of the Church. We've learned that protecting the Church's sacramental and spiritual integrity must be central to any operational change. While some business principles can be helpful, they must always serve, not replace, the Church's mission of evangelization, discipleship, and pastoral care.

The benefits of implementing and protecting the right system are well worth the effort. When a parish operates with a unified vision and a clear, consistent approach to management and ministry, the results can be truly transformative. Staff and volunteers feel empowered and motivated, knowing their work is making a real difference in the lives of those they serve. Parishioners experience a deeper sense of belonging and purpose, as they see the parish not just as a place to attend Mass but as a vibrant community of faith and mission.

Implementing the entire system also allows for a level of flexibility and adaptability that is essential in today's rapidly changing world. By having a clear framework in place, parishes can respond more nimbly to new challenges and opportunities without losing sight of their core mission and values.

We will explore each component of the system in greater depth, offering practical guidance and real-life examples of how parishes have successfully implemented these principles. We encourage you to approach this process with an open mind and a willing heart, trusting that God will guide and sustain you every step of the way.

Overview of the System

Here's an overview of the system we'll discuss throughout this book and how it can help align the business office, as well as the other parish teams, with the parish's mission. The system we propose consists of eight elements.

- ▸▸ **The Core** explores the fundamental elements that guide every successful parish: core values, mission, vision, long-term objectives, and a simplified strategy. These foundational components ensure that all decisions and efforts align with the Church's larger mission.

- ▸▸ Next, **Team Building** focuses on getting the right people in the right roles. This chapter delves into the importance of performance management, growing and developing staff, and building a team capable of advancing the parish's mission.

- ▸▸ In **Meeting People on the Path,** we discuss how to engage parishioners where they are on their faith journey. It emphasizes understanding their needs and providing support that helps guide them toward a deeper relationship with Christ. This needs to be the core process of your parish.

- ➤ **Using Process to Serve the Mission** illustrates how clearly defined processes are essential for a parish to function smoothly. Here, we explore how process management can be a tool for fulfilling the parish's mission rather than an end in itself. We offer some examples of the fundamental processes that can be used by parishes.

- ➤ **Project Management** highlights the importance of managing initiatives that have a clear beginning and end. Whether it's launching a new ministry or organizing a parish event, this chapter provides guidance on overseeing projects that contribute to the Church's goals.

- ➤ In **Parish Growth,** we turn our attention to measuring progress and outcomes. This chapter discusses how data can be used to assess how well the parish is performing in its mission and provides insights into making informed adjustments.

- ➤ **Problem Solving** covers the essential skills of decision-making, change management, and conflict resolution. Here, we explore how to address challenges that arise in parish life while keeping the focus on the mission.

- ➤ In the chapters **Alignment, and Putting it All Together,** we discuss how to integrate these principles into a cohesive approach that keeps the parish functioning in harmony, with all elements working toward the same goals. We show which order to apply these lessons, as compared to the logical way they're laid out in the chapters.

By implementing this system, parishes can create a culture of excellence, accountability, and shared purpose. They can ensure that every aspect of parish life, from the most mundane tasks to the most sacred moments, is oriented towards the ultimate goal of making disciples and building up the Body of Christ.

Consider Fr. Philip Brune's testimony of how implementing this book's strategies helped his parish: "I was first assigned as a pastor six years ago. I was excited to finally be able to make decisions and really serve the Church and our people in a more direct way, including the governance of the parish. To my surprise, it took me a year just to understand the flow of the parish and what was going on liturgically. There were so many people to meet, ministries to understand, and problems to solve. It took three years to know what kind of help I needed. Finally, by the fourth year, I started to understand the various components of the parish and how they could potentially work together, but many were not aligned. Finally, I was able to learn about this system and could then see clearly what had been missing those previous years: a clear framework that helped me grasp how the parish was supposed to work, which clearly highlighted the gaps I still had in my parish. Now I could find the root causes and then start solving issues rather than putting on bandaids. If I had this before I started, it would have saved me three years of flailing about searching for a unifying system." (Pastor, St. Robert Bellarmine, El Campo, TX)

Action Steps

1. **Pray:** Begin by asking the Holy Spirit to guide and inspire you as you seek to align your parish's business practices with its spiritual mission. Invite your staff, volunteers, and parishioners to join you in this prayer.

2. **Assess:** Take an honest look at your current parish management practices, identifying areas of strength and opportunities for growth. Use the insights from this chapter to help guide your assessment. Take the assessment in the workbook too.

3. **Dialogue:** Engage in open and honest conversations with your staff, volunteers, and parishioners about the vision for your parish and the role that each person plays in bringing that vision to life. Listen to their concerns, ideas, and aspirations.

4. **Plan:** Based on your assessment and dialogue, develop a clear plan for implementing the system outlined in this book. Break the plan down into manageable steps and assign a person and timelines for each step. Ask for help if you've never done this.

5. **Act:** Begin implementing your plan, starting with the Core, then Team and Strategy. Celebrate successes along the way and learn from any setbacks or challenges that arise.

03

The Administrative Core

Values, Mission/Vision, Long Term Objectives, Strategy Simplified

"

"Therefore, do not continue in ignorance, but try to understand what is the will of the Lord."

- - - -

EPHESIANS 5:17

The Core and the Journey

Preparing the administrative core for your organization is like preparing for a hike. When preparing for a hike, the first thing you do is decide your destination—that's your mission and vision. The destination represents a major milestone, the guiding purpose that shapes your administration for a period of time. Without choosing a clear destination, the hike and your team have no direction.

Next, you need to understand clearly where you are and choose your path from the available options—that's your strategy. The path represents the specific plan that will get you from here to there. Just like with any hike, there might be different routes, but the one you choose depends on your resources, your team, and the terrain. The mission drives your strategy, because the path you choose must align with your goal of reaching the summit. Be aware that misunderstanding your starting place can be problematic. We have seen many leaders sugarcoat their current situation, leading to poor path selection and putting their team in bad situations.

Once you've chosen your path, you need to determine how you'll organize your hike—that's your structure. You need to know who's carrying what, who's leading, and how the team will be arranged for safety and efficiency. The structure supports the strategy by ensuring everyone is positioned to succeed on the path. We'll talk about that in chapter 4.

Finally, your processes are like the steps you take on the hike. They're the day-to-day actions that get you moving forward. The way you take those steps—whether you walk steadily or sprint in short bursts—depends on the structure you've set up for your hike. In this way, mission drives strategy, strategy drives structure, and structure drives process. You'll see more on this in chapter 6.

In any organization, especially in a parish, this same dynamic applies. You choose the mission (the destination), the strategy (the path), the structure (the organization), and the processes (the steps). Together, they ensure that your journey is focused, efficient, and ultimately successful.

The Role of Core Values in an Organization

In *Built to Last: Successful Habits of Visionary Companies*, Jim Collins and Jerry I. Porras emphasize the significance of core values in shaping an organization's culture and success. They define core values as the fundamental and enduring principles that guide an organization's actions and decisions. The Church has enduring core values given to us directly by Jesus:

> *"He said to him, 'You shall love the Lord, your God, with all your heart, with all your soul, and with all your mind. This is the greatest and the first commandment. The second is like it: You shall love your neighbor as yourself."*
>
> **MATTHEW 22:37-39**

There are other directives Jesus gave us as well, but He says that these two are the core. Each parish will have its mission, which will evolve a little over time, but the core values remain unchanged. What this means, practically, is that each of the biblical virtues will be emphasized by each team member of a parish, informed by the parish's mission, the employee's job description, and the organization's focus at that moment in time. Each pastor (and lay leader) must help the team balance the tension of the biblical virtues as a management activity. For example, righteousness without humility and generosity does little to draw people toward Christ but runs the risk of pushing people away. Speaking wisdom with courage and integrity without patience and kindness runs the same risk. Kindness and generosity without integrity and courage might be a form of appeasement or coddling, not a form of agape love.

The workbook has an example of a handout that can be used for employees to remind them about their role in the Church's mission. Here we list the most important values that Jesus teaches his disciples.

➤ **Faith:** Trust and confidence in God, believing in His promises even without seeing immediate evidence. "Now faith is confidence in what we hope for and assurance about what we do not see." Hebrews 11:1

▸ **Hope:** A confident expectation of God's future goodness and faithfulness, even in times of hardship. "May the God of hope fill you with all joy and peace as you trust in him, so that you may overflow with hope by the power of the Holy Spirit." Romans 15:13

▸ **Love (Agape):** Selfless, sacrificial love that reflects God's love for humanity. "And now these three remain: faith, hope, and love. But the greatest of these is love." Corinthians 13:13

▸ **Humility:** A modest view of one's importance, recognizing dependence on God. "Do nothing out of selfish ambition or vain conceit. Rather, in humility, value others above yourselves." Philippians 2:3

▸ **Patience:** Enduring trials and waiting on God without complaint, showing grace in difficult circumstances. "You too, be patient and stand firm, because the Lord's coming is near." James 5:8

▸ **Kindness:** A gentle and compassionate attitude toward others, reflecting God's kindness to us "Be kind and compassionate to one another, forgiving each other, just as in Christ God forgave you." Ephesians 4:32

▸ **Generosity:** Willingness to give to others out of love, without expecting anything in return. "Each of you should give what you have decided in your heart to give, not reluctantly or under compulsion, for God loves a cheerful giver." 2 Corinthians 9:7

▸ **Forgiveness:** A readiness to forgive others as God has forgiven us. "Bear with each other and forgive one another if any of you has a grievance against someone. Forgive as the Lord forgave you." Colossians 3:13

▸ **Courage:** Boldness to stand firm in faith, especially in the face of danger or opposition. "Be strong and courageous. Do not be afraid; do not be discouraged, for the Lord your God will be with you wherever you go." Joshua 1:9

▸ **Integrity:** Living a life of honesty, uprightness, and moral purity, both in public and private. "Whoever walks in integrity walks securely, but whoever takes crooked paths will be found out." Proverbs 10:9

▸ **Peace (Shalom):** An inner sense of calm and well-being, rooted in a right relationship with God. "Blessed are the peacemakers, for they will be called children of God." Matthew 5:9

▸ **Wisdom:** The ability to make sound decisions and live rightly, guided by God's truth. "For the Lord gives wisdom; from his mouth come knowledge and understanding." Proverbs 2:6

▸ **Righteousness:** A commitment to doing what is right according to God's standards, reflecting moral purity and justice. "Blessed are those who hunger and thirst for righteousness, for they will be filled." Matthew 5:6

▸ **Self-Control:** Exercising discipline over one's desires and impulses, aligning them with God's will. "Be alert and of sober mind. Your enemy the devil prowls around like a roaring lion looking for someone to devour." 1 Peter 5:8

As a pastor, one of your primary responsibilities is to ensure that your parish operates in accordance with Jesus' set of core values. These values serve as the foundation for your parish's culture and provide a compass for navigating the challenges and opportunities you face. While no one lives these perfectly, we suggest you start by identifying where your leadership team is strongest and which ones you, they, and probably the rest of your parish need to work on. All together, these values will make up your parish's leadership principles.

Discovering and defining how the Church's core values are applied in your parish is a process that requires introspection, prayer, and discernment. It begins with you, as the leader, defining how the leadership principles operate in your parish in the context of your parish mission, always aligning with the values of the Church. Take time to reflect on the principles that guide your life and ministry, and be open to the Holy Spirit's guidance. The process of discerning the right principles for a parish typically takes at least two years, and that is when you are being very deliberate.

The next step is to make sure that you define clearly what each of these values should look like in behaviors. We call these Standards of Behavior, and when lived out consistently, they become the good habits, or virtues, that everyone lives together. You can find more details in the workbook.

Keep in mind that implementing leadership principles is an ongoing journey. As your parish grows and evolves, you may need to revisit and refine your values to ensure they continue to reflect Christ's teachings and the needs of your community over time and in different circumstances. You will certainly need to continue to shepherd your business office and wider parish towards the complete implementation of these principles in their work and lives.

How do we reconcile our imperfection with the need to imitate Jesus? The Church is a large tent in which everyone can and should be welcomed, yet the leadership

principles raise the bar to where our team is at currently as we strive to keep growing. So the expectation for anyone to be on the leadership team is that they are able to abide by these principles. Over time, this bar, and the corresponding expectations, should be raised higher and higher if we are growing as Jesus calls us to. This is why the apostles said that deacons should not be picked from recent converts: to give their fresh faith time to mature, deepen, and grow. Initially, your leadership principles, while never contrary to the Gospel values, might be much lower than you desire. However, as you change the mindset and raise the bar, the expectations can and should get closer to what Jesus calls us all towards.

Fr. Joe's story illustrates the challenges and importance of establishing clear values in a parish setting: When he transitioned from a small rural parish to a large urban one, he encountered a much more diverse staff with varying experiences and perspectives. He learned that, while involving others in the process is essential, he also needed to exercise his role as a leader to guide the discernment process and ensure that they had values aligned with the heart of the Gospel.

The Mission of the Church and Its Impact on Your Parish

As a Catholic parish, your mission is inherently tied to the mission of the universal Church. In Matthew 28:19-20, Jesus gave his disciples the Great Commission: "Go, therefore, and make disciples of all nations, baptizing them in the name of the Father, and of the Son, and of the Holy Spirit, teaching them to observe all that I have commanded you." This command is at the heart of the Church's mission and should be the driving force behind every Catholic parish.

Your parish's specific mission is a unique expression of how you live out the Great Commission in your particular context. Whether through education, healing, liturgical ministry, or other means, your parish is called to make disciples and lead people to Christ in its own distinctive way.

A mission statement answers the question, "What is our role in our community as a parish?" You start to understand the answer by looking at your diocesan mission or pastoral plan, your parish's history, the geography and demographics of people in your parish boundaries, and the needs of those we are currently serving and of those we're called to serve. The mission rarely changes from year to year but is not set in stone—it evolves at the call of the Holy Spirit.

Before writing a mission statement, consider your specific type of parish:

▸▸ Downtown cathedral, 100 years old, few parishioners live nearby, many young adults, daily Mass attendees who work downtown.

▸▸ Suburban parish, multiple generations, several cultures and languages, a strong community of key volunteers, and lots of young families.

▸▸ University parish, few stable parishioners, lots of students with few resources and time but a huge thirst for Jesus.

Keep in mind the various difficulties that your parish faces, as well as the general mission of the Church today: secularization, little interest in Jesus, and an epidemic of loneliness, etc.

Once the role of the parish is clear, developing a clear and compelling mission statement can help your parish stay focused on its purpose and priorities. A mission statement should be concise, memorable, and grounded in the language and imagery of the Great Commission. Here are a few examples:

▸▸ Make Disciples, Baptize, Teach, and Share Christ's Love (General Parish)

▸▸ Build Community, Transform Lives, Spread the Gospel (Urban Parish)

▸▸ Nurture Faith, Plant Seeds, Grow in Christ (Rural Parish)

▸▸ Strengthen Families, Baptize Souls, Guide in Faith (Family-Oriented Parish)

Notice how each of these mission statements includes action-oriented verbs that align with the call to make disciples, deepen through formation, and become an apostle. They also reflect the unique context and focus of each parish community.

As you work to clarify your parish's mission, involve your staff, volunteers, and parishioners in the process. Engage them in prayerful discernment, asking the Holy Spirit to guide your conversations and reveal God's will for your community. By collaborating with others in defining your mission, you foster a sense of shared ownership and commitment to living out that mission together.

Once you have a clear mission statement, the next step is to ensure that every aspect of your parish life reflects and supports that mission. This includes your liturgies, ministries, religious education programs, service projects, school if you have one, and even your budgetary and staffing decisions. When your mission is fully integrated into the life of your parish, it has the power to transform lives and draw people into a deeper relationship with Christ. Keep in mind that getting this level of clarity sometimes takes more than a day of discernment; it might take a year or more.

Your mission is not just a statement on a wall or a page in a bulletin. It is a living call to participate in the very mission of Christ and His Church. By rooting your parish's mission in the Great Commission and integrating it into every aspect of your community's life, you can become a vibrant, fruitful center of discipleship and evangelization.

Strategy: The Path Forward

At its core, strategy is the plan you use to achieve your mission. It's the deliberate choice of actions, priorities, and resources that guide how your parish moves toward fulfilling its calling. While mission tells you why you're doing something, strategy tells you how you will get it done. In this sense, strategy is not just about what you will do—it's also about what you won't do.

Peter Drucker, often referred to as the father of modern management, said, "Strategy is a form of denial." This means that an effective strategy requires focus and a clear understanding that you cannot do everything. Strategy forces you to make tough choices about where to allocate resources—time, talent, and treasure—based on what will most effectively move the parish toward its mission. In a parish setting, this is particularly important because you're dealing with limited resources and diverse needs. Without a clear strategy, a parish can get spread too thin, trying to serve every need without doing any of it well.

Strategy in a Parish Context

For a parish, strategy takes on a unique dimension because your mission is rooted in faith, evangelization, and community building. While businesses may focus on profits, parishes must focus on spiritual outcomes—forming disciples, fostering community, and facilitating encounters with Christ. The challenge is that these outcomes can be harder to quantify, and the resources needed to achieve them are often in short supply.

This is where strategy becomes crucial. In a parish, your strategy will guide how you:

▸▸ **Prioritize ministries and services:** Which ministries will get the most resources, and which ones might be put on hold or scaled back?

▸▸ **Allocate budget and time:** How will the parish invest its limited financial resources and staff/volunteer hours?

▸▸ **Engage your community:** Which groups of parishioners or outreach efforts should be your primary focus?

▸▸ **Support diocesan goals:** If your diocese has a clear strategy, the parish's strategy should align with it. The diocese provides the broader vision for how the Church is operating in your region, and your parish is a key player in fulfilling that vision.

For example, if your diocese has made evangelization a priority—focusing on reaching out to inactive Catholics or non-Catholics—then your parish strategy should reflect this by prioritizing outreach and evangelization efforts. This might mean dedicating resources to community events, OCIA programs, or online engagement. The goal is to ensure that your parish strategy is not working in isolation but is in sync with the larger Church's goals

A Simple Framework for Choosing Your Strategy

There is a library full of books (and as many post-graduate degrees) that discuss strategy. We've attached a straightforward approach that includes hundreds of years of strategic thinking and resolves it with the best book on management ever written: the Bible. Choosing a parish strategy can feel overwhelming, but breaking it down into clear steps can make the process more manageable. If you get stuck, focus on the next decision that must be made.

Clarify the Mission and Vision: The strategy must flow directly from your mission. What is your parish's specific mission, and how does it fit into the broader mission of the Church and your diocese? Your strategy should help you live out that mission in a practical, focused way.

▸▸ **Evaluate Your Resources:** Take stock of the resources available to your parish. What is your budget? How many staff or volunteers do you have?

What ministries are already operating, and how effective are they? Understanding your resource limits will help you make realistic choices about what is possible.

▸▸ **Identify Key Opportunities and Challenges:** Look at the internal and external environments. Are there opportunities in your community for outreach? Are there unmet spiritual needs in the parish? What challenges do you face—such as limited financial resources or declining participation?

▸▸ **Make Deliberate Choices:** This is where Drucker's principle of "denial" comes into play. Decide what not to do. This could mean narrowing your focus to a few key ministries, eliminating programs that are not contributing to the mission, or choosing to concentrate on one demographic, such as young families or seniors. By being selective, you give your parish the focus it needs to succeed. Keep in mind that there will be short-term and long-term areas of focus, but the areas of the parish administrative operations are always people, finances, parish operations, and fundraising. (See chapter 11 for more detail.)

▸▸ **Align with Diocesan Strategy:** If the diocese has its own strategy, your parish must align with it. Talk to your diocesan leadership, review diocesan goals, and make sure your strategy fits within that framework. If your parish's strategy contradicts diocesan goals, it can cause friction and undermine both efforts.

▸▸ **Set Measurable Objectives:** Every strategy must be accompanied by measurable objectives. How will you know if your parish is on or off plan? For example, if your strategy focuses on evangelization, set concrete goals such as increasing the number of baptisms or participants in OCIA or boosting attendance at Mass. These goals give you a way to track progress and adjust your strategy if needed.

▸▸ **Communicate the Strategy:** Once your strategy is clear, communicate it widely. Staff, volunteers, and parishioners need to know where the parish is headed and why. When people understand the strategy, they can align their own efforts to help achieve it.

▸▸ **Review and Adjust:** Strategy is not static. Regularly review how your parish is progressing toward its goals. Is the strategy working, or do adjustments need to be made? Are you on track with your long-term objectives? This review process ensures that your strategy remains relevant as conditions change.

Measuring Success: Are We On Or Off Plan?

One of the most important aspects of strategy is measurement, which we'll cover more in depth in chapter 9. Without clear metrics, you won't know whether your strategy is working. In the corporate world, this might be measured by profits or customer satisfaction, but in a parish, success looks different. The key is to tie your metrics to your mission. In chapter 8, we will discuss the importance of measuring the parish in detail.

By setting clear objectives and regularly measuring progress, you can keep your parish on course and adjust as necessary. Measurement is key not just for keeping on track but for ensuring that the resources of the parish are being stewarded well and are directly contributing to the mission.

By combining prayerful discernment, wise planning, and trust in God's guidance, your parish can develop a strategic vision that will bear fruit for years to come. Your long-term goals and plans will become a roadmap for living out your mission and making a lasting impact in your community and the world.

Long-Term Goals: Setting the Course for the Parish

Long-term goals are the milestones that guide your parish toward fulfilling its mission. They are the high-level objectives that provide direction for where you want to be in the next three to five years. The challenge is finding the balance between setting goals that are clear and measurable without being so specific that they limit flexibility or stifle creativity. A parish, after all, is a living, breathing community, not a rigid institution. As Michael Gerber emphasizes in The E-Myth, your organization must be able to adapt and evolve without losing sight of its core mission.

Drawing inspiration from Peter Drucker's principle that "what gets measured gets managed," long-term goals must be measurable. However, they should remain high-level enough to allow flexibility in how they are achieved. W. Edwards Deming, credited with revolutionizing Japan's industry after WWII, also reminds us that goals are not just about hitting targets; they should be part of a system that continuously improves and adapts. This system should ensure that progress can be reviewed regularly, adjustments can be made, and the entire parish remains aligned with the mission.

For a parish, this means that your long-term goals must be broad enough to capture the big picture but also connected to the day-to-day actions that make progress possible. Here's how you can set goals that work for the long term while still keeping the parish on track for today.

Setting Long-Term Goals: The Balance Between Vision and Flexibility

When setting long-term goals for your parish, think of them as guiding markers rather than specific tasks. They should be clear enough to direct your focus but not so detailed that they choke innovation or restrict necessary adaptations. A good long-term goal is ambitious and measurable but leaves room for how it will be achieved.

For example, instead of setting a goal that says, "Increase Mass attendance by 20% within three years," consider a broader, more flexible goal like: "Increase parish engagement and participation over the next three years." This allows your team to set measurable objectives such as Mass attendance, participation in ministries, and outreach programs, but it also leaves room for changes in strategy depending on what works and what doesn't. You're focusing on the outcome (engagement) without micromanaging the exact path to get there.

The key is to make your goals actionable but adaptable. You need to ask, "If this is where we want to be in three to five years, what do we need to do this year, this quarter, and today to stay on track?" We will discuss this further in chapters 6 and 9.

Developing a strategic plan is a significant accomplishment, but the real work begins with implementation. As you put your plan into action, it's essential to keep in mind the long-term sustainability of your efforts. You want to ensure that your parish's mission and ministries can thrive not just in the short term but for generations to comeIntegrating Faith, Values, Mission, and Strategy

When we do the hard work of integration, the fruits can be truly abundant. We create parishes that are not simply places of worship, but vibrant communities of missionary disciples, committed to living out the Gospel in every aspect of their lives.

As pastoral leaders, this is our highest calling and our greatest challenge - to create communities that radiate the love, mercy, and truth of Jesus Christ to a world in need. By staying grounded in faith, guided by values, focused on mission, and committed to strategic vision, we can rise to this challenge and lead our parishes towards a future of hope and renewal.

> *"For I know the plans I have for you,' declares the Lord, 'plans to prosper you and not to harm you, plans to give you hope and a future."*
>
> **JEREMIAH 29:11**

Action Steps

1. Identify the current culture of your parish, starting with your leadership team, key volunteers and ministries, and the parishioners.

2. Analyze which ones are positive values that reflect the Gospel values and what areas are unhealthy and need to change.

3. Put together the Gospel values plus your parish's positive values to make a list of leadership principles to guide your parish culture.

04

CHAPTER

Building Your Pastoral Team

The Cornerstone of Parish Leadership

Father Michael stood at the altar, his hands trembling slightly as he prepared to celebrate his first Mass as the new pastor of St. Catherine's. As he looked out at his parishioners' faces - some curious, others expectant - a verse from Scripture echoed in his mind:

> *"I have become all things to all, to save at least some. All this I do for the sake of the gospel, so that I too may have a share in it."*
>
> **1 CORINTHIANS 9:22-23**

Little did Father Michael know that these words from St. Paul would become the foundation of his approach to building a pastoral team. In the following weeks and months, he would learn that effective parish leadership requires a delicate balance of adapting to diverse roles while maintaining an unwavering focus on the Gospel mission. Some of his parish team were full-time paid staff members, some were part-time, and then he found a group of dedicated volunteers. Overall, there seemed to be little clarity, and he wasn't even sure what everyone was doing most of the time.

Over time, he realized that it was hard to get people to agree on what the priorities were, and he started to wonder if his job was to make saints or run a business. The responsibilities of managing a parish can feel overwhelming, especially when you're trying to balance the spiritual needs of your flock with the practical demands of running what is often a medium-to-large-size organization.

Building a strong pastoral team is not just about finding people to handle tasks; it's about creating a family united in Christ's mission. It's about embodying St. Paul's adaptability and becoming "all things to all" to advance the Gospel while addressing your parish's practical needs.

It is also about getting tasks done well. Think of your pastoral team as a living embodiment of the acronym T.E.A.M. - Together Everyone Achieves Mission. This simple phrase encapsulates a profound truth: the collaborative nature of parish work, where each member contributes their unique gifts to fulfill the Church's mission.

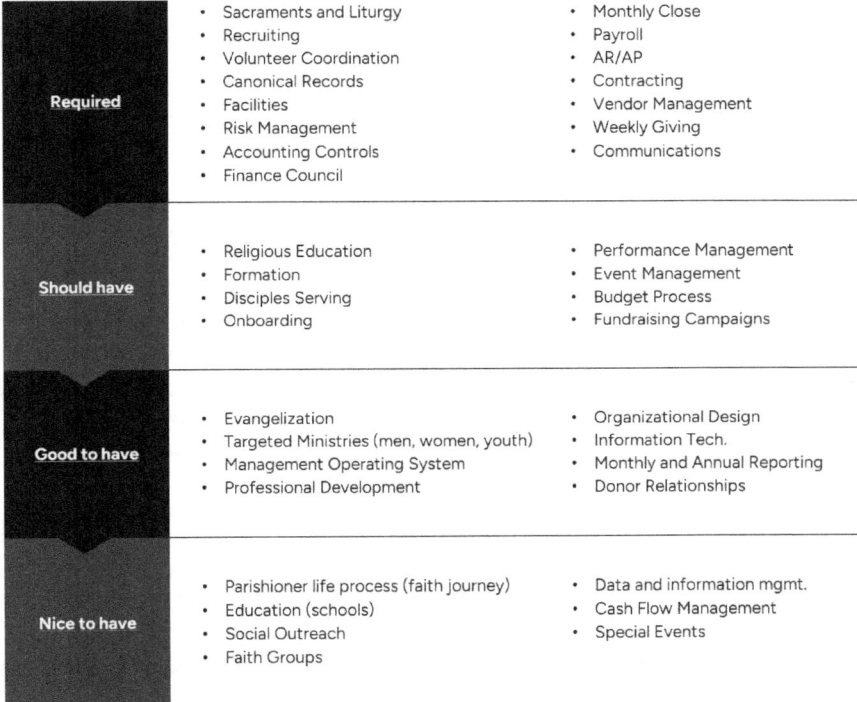

Required	• Sacraments and Liturgy • Recruiting • Volunteer Coordination • Canonical Records • Facilities • Risk Management • Accounting Controls • Finance Council	• Monthly Close • Payroll • AR/AP • Contracting • Vendor Management • Weekly Giving • Communications
Should have	• Religious Education • Formation • Disciples Serving • Onboarding	• Performance Management • Event Management • Budget Process • Fundraising Campaigns
Good to have	• Evangelization • Targeted Ministries (men, women, youth) • Management Operating System • Professional Development	• Organizational Design • Information Tech. • Monthly and Annual Reporting • Donor Relationships
Nice to have	• Parishioner life process (faith journey) • Education (schools) • Social Outreach • Faith Groups	• Data and information mgmt. • Cash Flow Management • Special Events

It's also important to recognize that you're part of a larger trend in the Church. According to a 2019 study by the Center for Applied Research in the Apostolate, 66% of U.S. parishes employ lay staff members. This statistic underscores the growing importance of effective team management for modern pastors and highlights the need to develop skills in working with lay professionals while maintaining your parish's spiritual focus.

As we delve into the intricacies of building your pastoral team, we'll explore practical strategies grounded in spiritual principles. We'll discuss how to structure your team, recruit the right people, meet them where they are, and manage performance in a way that honors professional standards and your parish's mission. Ultimately, being pastoral also means holding your team to higher standards than the average parishioner because they are called to be an extension of you. It is poor stewardship

of the parish resources to keep people who are not capable of doing their job, and it's uncharitable to the individual to keep them in a role where they are not thriving.

Throughout this journey, keep in mind this affirmation: "With God's grace, I build and nurture a team that serves our parish and community with love, efficiency, and a shared commitment to our gospel mission." Let this be your guiding light as we explore the path of building a strong, effective pastoral team.

Structuring a Parish Team

Similar to the way an architect designs a building with a framework that strives to meet the needs of the final user, a pastor needs to design a pastoral team using a basic framework that meets the practical and spiritual needs of the parish community. As in a building, there are some elements that are more fundamental than others. The foundation and roof are more essential than flooring and lights, and those are also more important than furnishings and artwork.

Structuring a parish team requires balancing the Church's canonical requirements with the unique realities of each parish, whether the parish is in the early stages of growth, thriving, or facing struggles. While every parish has its own circumstances, certain elements are universal as outlined in the graphic below. The important point is that each of these must be handled by someone who is specifically assigned and that the most important tasks must be handled before adding less critical tasks.

The stage of growth of a parish must also be considered when it comes to creating the right team structure. Here are some examples of those different stages:

- ▶▶ **Upstart parishes** often have limited resources and a smaller staff. In these settings, team members wear multiple hats, and roles may be more fluid. The team's structure is often lean, relying heavily on volunteers and cross-functional roles, with the pastor taking on a direct and visible leadership role in both spiritual and administrative matters.

- ▶▶ **Growing parishes** begin to see an expansion in ministries and a need for more specialized roles. As the parish grows, roles become more defined. For example, you might need a full-time director of religious education or a dedicated development coordinator to manage increasing demands for catechesis and fundraising efforts. This is also the stage where the need for stronger management systems and clear lines of authority becomes more pressing.

▸ **Thriving parishes** typically have more resources and larger staffs. Here, the structure tends to mirror that of a more complex organization, with dedicated roles for each ministry, more robust financial management, and clear systems for communication and decision-making. While the pastor remains the ultimate authority, much of the day-to-day administration may be delegated to staff members, allowing the pastor to focus on spiritual leadership.

▸ **Struggling parishes**, on the other hand, may need to consolidate roles and focus on survival strategies. In these cases, team structure often involves a reassessment of priorities, with an emphasis on core ministries. The finance council might focus on crisis management, while the pastoral council works on identifying the parish's most pressing needs and opportunities for renewal.

Parish Leadership Groups

Canonical requirements ensure that key roles like the pastor and finance council are always in place, but the day-to-day operations and team structure need to reflect the unique stage and circumstances of the parish. Balancing these elements is critical to leading a parish effectively, regardless of its current phase of development. Now we want to give some helpful ideas on the basic parish groups and how they can serve the parish mission well.

Councils

The **finance council,** mandated by Canon 537, advises the pastor on financial matters and ensures proper stewardship of parish resources. This council is particularly important in parishes experiencing financial strain or growth, where fiscal responsibility becomes critical to sustaining ministry. In a struggling parish, the finance council might focus on prioritizing resources and finding ways to stabilize finances. In a thriving parish, they may be more focused on strategic growth initiatives or long-term investments. In any case, the finance council's effectiveness is directly linked to the accuracy of the information they are given. This information flow does not need to be a heavy reporting lift but instead should be a view of the

parish through the lens of the pastor with transparency. This will lead to the best council, discourse, and debate from which the pastor can make decisions.

Another common structure, though not canonically required everywhere, is the **pastoral council**. This body serves as an advisory group to the pastor, helping guide decisions around the spiritual and community life of the parish. Like the finance council, the parish council can only offer guidance based on the information they have. One benefit of a well-run, diverse parish council is the opportunity for each of the members to see the parish through the eyes of other members to understand the implication of the decisions that the pastor is faced with. A high-functioning parish council is varied in their backgrounds, professional and personal experiences, parish involvement and engagement.

Some parishes have other councils or committees based on their needs. These might be to help manage a building project, fundraising, putting on a large event like a parish picnic or fiesta, or other specific needs. In all cases, these groups should be given sufficient guidance and leadership to operate most effectively as advisors to the pastor. The more clarity they have on their roles and responsibilities, the purpose and desired outcomes of upcoming meetings, and the reports and information they need, preferably well before meetings, the more likely they are to serve the needs of the parish and the pastor well.

The Parish Office

Beyond the pastor, finance council, and pastoral council, a well-functioning parish relies on a broader team that includes both staff and volunteers. The structure of this team can vary significantly depending on the parish's size and stage of development, but certain roles and functions are essential to every parish, whether it's upstart, growing, thriving, or struggling.

The **parish office** serves as the administrative backbone. This is where the day-to-day operations are managed, and it typically includes a range of roles such as office managers, administrative assistants, and sometimes specialized roles like development or communication coordinators. The parish office handles everything from managing sacramental records to scheduling events, maintaining the parish database, and ensuring smooth communication with parishioners.

In **upstart parishes,** the parish office may be minimal, often consisting of a single office manager or administrative assistant who handles multiple responsibilities. This person is often the lifeline of the parish's operations, doing everything from answering phones and maintaining records to coordinating volunteers and managing the pastor's schedule. The team here is typically lean, with individuals taking on broad roles to keep everything running smoothly.

In **growing parishes,** the office starts to expand. As the needs of the parish increase, specialized roles emerge. A communications coordinator might be brought on to handle newsletters, social media, and parish-wide announcements. A development officer could manage fundraising campaigns and stewardship programs. At this stage, the office must become more organized, with clearer job descriptions and delineated responsibilities to handle the growing complexity of parish operations.

For **thriving parishes**, the office might resemble a small business in its complexity, with distinct departments or teams focusing on different areas—communication, development, administration, and event coordination. These parishes often have dedicated staff members for liturgical planning, facilities management, and ministry coordination. This allows the pastor and leadership team to focus more on spiritual leadership while day-to-day operations are managed by professional staff.

In **struggling parishes**, the office may be pared down to its essentials, with a focus on efficiency and cost-saving measures. In these situations, one or two staff members may need to handle a wide range of duties, requiring flexibility and a "do-it-all" attitude. Here, the pastor often takes on a more hands-on administrative role, and volunteers may be called upon to fill gaps left by a smaller staff.

Volunteers

Volunteers are the lifeblood of most parishes, often making up the bulk of the team responsible for ministries, events, and outreach programs. Their involvement can range from liturgical roles (such as lectors, Extraordinary Ministers of Holy Communion, and altar servers) to administrative and operational support (such as organizing parish events or maintaining the grounds). The key to successfully managing volunteers is ensuring that their work aligns with the parish's mission while providing them with the support and training they need to thrive.

In **upstart parishes,** volunteers often play a central role in everything, from running catechesis programs to coordinating events. With limited resources, an upstart parish relies heavily on the commitment and energy of its volunteers. The challenge here is to recruit dedicated individuals who can take ownership of key responsibilities and to foster a culture of collaboration and mission-driven service. Since volunteers may need to take on roles that would typically be handled by paid staff in larger parishes, the pastor and leadership team must be actively involved in recruiting, training, and supporting them.

In **growing parishes,** the role of volunteers begins to formalize. As more ministries develop, volunteers need clearer direction, training, and supervision. At this stage, having a volunteer coordinator or ministry leader to organize, support, and communicate with volunteers becomes essential. Volunteers in these parishes often lead key initiatives like youth programs, adult faith formation, and community outreach efforts. Ensuring that they feel valued and equipped is crucial to sustaining their involvement.

For **thriving parishes,** volunteers are often abundant, and their roles are highly structured. These parishes may have formal onboarding processes for volunteers, training programs, and systems for tracking volunteer hours and responsibilities. The goal in a thriving parish is not just to engage volunteers but to empower them as leaders within the parish community. Volunteers may even be given substantial autonomy in certain ministries, with staff providing oversight and support where needed.

In **struggling parishes,** volunteers often take on greater responsibility as the parish works to do more with less. Here, volunteers may need to step into roles typically filled by paid staff, such as helping with administrative tasks, managing facilities, or leading significant ministry efforts. In such cases, providing volunteers with clear direction, support, and recognition is critical to prevent burnout and maintain engagement. The challenge for the leadership is to keep volunteers motivated and aligned with the parish's mission, even during difficult times

Balancing Professional Staff and Volunteers

The relationship between professional staff and volunteers is vital to a parish's success. As we mentioned before, the small amount of priests and the large numbers of laity require lots of collaborators in the mission. In a very small parish, the pastor might be the only one who is paid, with a couple of volunteers to help. Generally, as a parish grows, the need for and ability to pay for full-time staff increases. However, the number of volunteers shouldn't decrease; rather, they too should grow. In any parish, the pastor must ensure that staff and volunteers are working together harmoniously, with clear lines of communication and shared expectations. Volunteers often bring passion, while staff bring professional expertise and consistency. Both are essential. The pastor and leadership team should create an environment where both groups feel valued and supported.

In some cases, particularly in growing and thriving parishes, there may be tension between staff and volunteers regarding authority, responsibility, and decision-making. It's important to establish clear boundaries: staff should not feel threatened by volunteers, and volunteers should not feel marginalized by staff. A well-structured team fosters collaboration between both, ensuring that the mission of the parish remains the focus.

Assembling a High-Performing Team

While Jesus personally chose each of his disciples, most pastors find an existing staff and are encouraged to not make any changes right away. Sometimes you need to make changes more urgently, and over time, you can shape the team more due to natural attrition. Forming your parish team is not merely about filling positions; it's about inviting individuals to participate in a sacred mission. Let's explore how to approach this crucial task with spiritual discernment and practical wisdom.

Before you cast your net, you need to know what you're fishing for. Creating **comprehensive job descriptions** is your first step. These should blend professional skills with ministry goals, clearly outlining how each role contributes to the parish's mission. Each job description should start with an overview of the parish. Next, you will outline the job responsibilities, focusing on the five most important aspects of the job and how each is measured for success. Be sure that each of the responsibilities identified above lands on someone's job description.

What about compensation? While we work towards the coming of God's Kingdom, we must also recognize the practical needs of our team members. Strive to balance market rates with budget constraints. This might mean getting creative with benefits that reflect Catholic social teaching. Consider offering flexible schedules to

accommodate family life, providing opportunities for spiritual retreats, or offering tuition assistance for children attending Catholic schools. These benefits can make a position attractive and competitive in the marketplace even if the salary isn't at the top of the market range.

That said, as a Church, we need to strive to pay closer to market rates, both to be true to Catholic social teaching and to provide a better service to our parishioners who are supporting this work with their donations. Paying someone more doesn't make them more effective, but a competitive wage does allow you to attract and retain better talent. Sometimes paying twice as much gets you three or four times the benefit to the parish. As pastor, it isn't your task to give people jobs. Your mission is to get people to Heaven by using the parish resources wisely.

Sourcing and Screening

When it comes to finding candidates, cast your net wide but strategically. Leverage diocesan resources and Catholic job boards. Don't underestimate the power of your parish network - announce openings at Mass and in your bulletin. You might be surprised to find talented parishioners eager to use their professional skills in service of the Church.

As you screen candidates, start with the resume, but know that the story is ultimately more important than the bullet points. Develop a screening process that assesses skills and cultural fit. Be wise about what you are looking for. We once met a leader who wanted to screen out an applicant for a blue-collar position due to the misspellings on the job application. Screening out for lack of skills that have no bearing on the job is a common mistake made by leaders inside the church and out.

The Interview: Discerning Fit And Culture

The interview process is your opportunity to discern not just competency but also cultural and spiritual fit. Psychologically, if you see someone who has the heart for the mission and gets along well with the team, your gut has already made a decision before you have analyzed if they can fulfill the job well. To avoid this, analyze their job skills first. If you're not competent in the area you're hiring for, which is normal if you're trying to hire talented people, use other qualified people to help in this process. Only after you determine they can do the job should you analyze if they align with your parish's mission and values. Both skills and culture are equally important, but the interview process needs to evaluate the ability to do the job before the cultural fit.

In the interview process, use behavioral questions to evaluate how candidates have handled situations in the past. For example, ask, "Can you tell me about a time when you had to make a difficult ethical decision in your professional life? How did your faith inform your choice?" Another important question, especially for ministry positions is, "Can you tell me about your relationship with Jesus?" If they are not able to articulate it clearly or only talk about the institutional Church, they might be lacking some important evangelization tools.

Also, keep in mind the next paragraph when you're looking for expertise that is outside of your own. You might need to bring in an interview panel from outside the parish for certain roles when you're not capable of analyzing their skillset.

Don't shy away from discussing faith during the interview. This is not unlawful discrimination in a faith-based organization. Ask candidates about their spiritual journey and how they see their work as an extension of their faith. Remember, you're looking for team members who will not just perform tasks but who will embody the mission of your parish in their work.

Sealing The Deal: Offers And Onboarding

Once you've found the right person, craft an offer letter that goes beyond salary and start date. Clearly outline expectations, responsibilities, and growth opportunities. Make it clear that joining your team means becoming part of a faith community dedicated to serving God and others.

Design a 30-60-90-day onboarding plan that integrates new hires into both their role and the parish community. This might include:

▸ A welcome Mass where you introduce the new team member to the parish

▸ Meetings with key ministry leaders to understand the parish's various activities

▸ A day of service alongside parishioners to connect with the community

▸ Regular check-ins to discuss job performance and spiritual growth

Effective onboarding isn't just about job training; it's about helping new team members find their place in your parish family.

> *"The harvest is abundant, but the laborers are few; so ask the master of the harvest to send out laborers for his harvest"*
>
> MATTHEW 9:37-38

By approaching recruitment with this blend of spiritual discernment and practical strategy, you're not just hiring employees - you're inviting disciples to join you in the vital work of parish ministry. You're building a team that will support you in your pastoral duties while ensuring the smooth operation of your parish.

Managing Experts Outside of Your Expertise

As a priest, you're often responsible for overseeing areas of parish life that fall outside your immediate expertise—finances, legal matters, facilities management, technology, and communications, to name a few. While you're not expected to master these fields, you are expected to hire and manage the people who have that expertise effectively. This requires a unique set of skills, including asking the right questions, ensuring alignment with the mission of the parish, and implementing clear management practices.

Trusting Expertise, Asking "Why?" Five Times

When working with experts outside your area of knowledge, one of the most valuable tools you have is the ability to ask questions. It's easy to defer to experts when they present a solution, but your role is to ensure that their work serves the parish's mission, not just solves a technical problem. Asking "Why?" multiple times—ideally five—helps uncover the root cause of any issue or recommendation. This technique, popularized by W. Edwards Deming and used in problem-solving across industries, is critical in ensuring that the decisions being made truly address the underlying needs of your parish.

For example, imagine a facilities manager recommends a costly upgrade to the parish's heating system. Instead of immediately approving or rejecting it, start by asking "Why?"

Why do we need to upgrade the system?

Because the current system is inefficient.

Why is it inefficient?

Because it's outdated and consumes more energy than newer models.

Why does that matter to us right now?

Because energy costs are rising, and this system is straining our budget.

Why can't we find a short-term solution to lower costs?

Short-term fixes won't address the underlying problem of an aging system that is likely to break down soon.

Why should this be a priority over other necessary projects?

Because if the system fails in the middle of winter, it will lead to emergency repairs and greater disruption to the parish's operations.

By asking "Why?" repeatedly, you move past surface-level answers and get to the root of the issue, allowing you to make more informed decisions. In this case, you discover that the upgrade is not just about inefficiency but about preventing future costly emergencies. This process helps ensure that decisions made by experts are aligned with the parish's broader goals and mission, not just immediate technical concerns. If an employee or expert cannot provide clarity upon multiple levels of questions, they might not be as capable as you thought they were.

Managing Experts with Clear Accountability

Another key to managing experts effectively is ensuring that every task, recommendation, or project they bring to you is accompanied by clear next steps, a due date, and a responsible party. This management tool, also known as "Who, What, and When," ensures accountability and keeps projects moving forward. While experts may bring solutions, it's your responsibility to ensure those solutions are executed properly, with measurable progress.

For example, after approving the heating system upgrade, you need to make sure the project is followed through. The next step might look like this:

▸ **What:** Finalize vendor selection for heating system replacement

▸ **Who:** Facilities manager

▸ **When:** By the end of the month

By assigning clear responsibilities, deadlines, and action items, you ensure that nothing falls through the cracks. As the parish leader, your role is to check in on these steps and follow up as needed. It's not enough to approve a plan—you must ensure that the work is being done on time and by the appropriate person.

This management practice also extends to meetings with your experts. Every meeting should result in concrete next steps, each with a designated person responsible and a clear deadline. This form of management, while simple, ensures that all parties remain focused and accountable, and it prevents delays caused by unclear expectations. We will cover this management technique more thoroughly in **Chapter 10: Alignment,** but it's a foundational tool for ensuring that your expert advisors are not just providing advice but delivering results.

Building Relationships with Experts

To effectively manage experts, you must also build strong, trusting relationships with them. While you might not share their technical knowledge, you are the one who defines the parish's mission and ensures that all work supports that mission. Experts need to feel that their knowledge is respected but also understand that their solutions must align with the spiritual and operational goals of the parish.

Good relationships with experts are built on clear communication and mutual respect. When experts present their recommendations, listen carefully, ask questions to clarify anything you don't understand, and then bring the conversation back to how their work serves the parish's broader mission. When they feel valued and heard, they will be more engaged in the work. But also ensure that they understand your role as the ultimate decision-maker, responsible for maintaining the mission focus.

Clear communication also means setting boundaries. While you need to respect their expertise, you should not be afraid to question or redirect their efforts when necessary. Managing experts effectively is a balancing act between delegating authority and retaining oversight.

Staying Focused on the Parish Mission

No matter how technical or operational the decisions are, they must always be made in the context of the parish's mission. Experts often come to the table with solutions that make sense from a technical standpoint, but it's your responsibility to ensure that their recommendations align with the spiritual and pastoral goals of the parish.

For example, if a communications expert suggests a new digital communication campaign to boost parish donations, your first concern should be how that campaign aligns with the parish's mission of fostering spiritual growth and engagement. Does the campaign reflect the values of the parish? Will it enhance the community's connection to the Church, or does it risk feeling overly transactional? These are the kinds of questions you must continually ask to ensure that experts are contributing to the parish's larger goals.

Performance Management

> *"Well done, my good and faithful servant."*
>
> **MATTHEW 25:21**

These words from the parable of the talents resonate deeply as we consider the delicate task of managing performance within a parish setting. As a pastor, you're called to be both a spiritual shepherd and an effective leader, guiding your team to fulfill their potential in service of your parish's mission

Let's explore a framework that blends professional management techniques with pastoral care: the **Five Box Management Plan.** This approach adapts corporate tools to the unique context of parish life, ensuring that your team members grow professionally and spiritually.

1. **Job Description Summary:** Just as Jesus gave clear instructions to His disciples, provide your team with well-defined goals and responsibilities. These should align with their job descriptions and the parish's overall mission. For example, your business administrator's goals might include not just financial targets but also how their work supports specific ministry initiatives.

2. **Objectives and Measures of Success:** Regular check-ins are crucial. These aren't just about task completion but about nurturing growth. Use

these times to offer praise and constructive criticism, always framed within the context of your shared mission. A simple question like, "How do you see your work contributing to our parish's goals this week?" can spark meaningful dialogue.

3.   **Formal Reviews:** While ongoing feedback is important, formal performance reviews provide a structured opportunity for deeper reflection. Conduct these semi-annually or annually, focusing not just on job performance but on how the team member is living out the parish's values in their work.

4.   **Development Plans:** Work with each team member to create personalized growth plans. These should address professional skills and spiritual formation. For instance, a plan for your youth minister might include attending a diocesan leadership workshop and participating in a parish Bible study.

5.   **Connecting to Who We Serve and Impact in Our Job:** This list reminds the team of the impact we have on the people around us. It is helpful when considering our work and the unintended consequences of our actions.

Implementing this plan requires a delicate balance of managerial skill and pastoral sensitivity. When providing feedback, especially constructive criticism, approach the conversation with empathy and grace. Frame your feedback in terms of growth and alignment with the parish's mission, rather than mere criticism.

For example, instead of saying, "Your reports are always late," try, "I've noticed the finance committee is struggling to make decisions because they don't have timely information. How can we work together to ensure they have what they need to be good stewards of our resources?"

When having difficult conversations, remember that you're not just addressing a performance issue; you're guiding a fellow disciple. Start with prayer, asking for wisdom and compassion. Listen actively, seeking to understand any underlying issues or obstacles. Together, develop an action plan that addresses the concern while supporting the team member's overall growth and well-being.

Evaluating Performance through a Coaching Lens

When evaluating performance, it's helpful to take a coaching approach, where performance is seen as the result of four factors: skill, effort, prioritization, and mindset. This framework not only helps you diagnose where someone may be struggling but also helps you tailor your response in a way that fosters growth.

▸▸ **Skill:** Sometimes poor performance stems from a lack of skill or experience. In these cases, training, coaching, and practice are necessary for development. For example, if your music director is struggling with organizing choir rehearsals, it might not be a matter of effort but rather a lack of training in leadership or time management.

▸▸ **Effort:** If the issue is effort or accountability, it's appropriate to address this with direct and firm feedback. Lack of effort usually calls for discipline or redirection, as it reflects a failure to take responsibility for one's work. Here, you can challenge team members by encouraging them to live up to their commitments but always in the context of grace and forgiveness.

▸▸ **Prioritization:** Sometimes the problem is not skill or effort but simply a misunderstanding of priorities. A team member might be working hard but on tasks that aren't as critical. In this case, discussions around prioritization are key, and this will be explored further in chapters 9 and 10. Through dialogue, you can help realign their focus to ensure that their energy is directed toward what matters most for the parish.

▸▸ **Mindset:** Occasionally, a team member's mindset or attitude may be the limiting factor. Changing someone's mindset requires more than a one-time conversation; it involves consistent reinforcement, journaling, and personal reflection, as we'll discuss in the workbook. By helping team members reflect on their motivations and approach, you guide them toward deeper personal growth that impacts their professional and spiritual lives.

Aligning Efforts with the Parish Mission

Aligning team efforts with parish mission and goals is an ongoing process. Regular team meetings are an excellent opportunity to reinforce this connection. Start each meeting with a brief reflection on how your work relates to the parish's mission. Encourage team members to share stories of how their work has positively impacted the community.

Setting SMART goals (Specific, Measurable, Achievable, Relevant, Time-bound) that reflect operational needs and spiritual objectives can provide clear direction. For instance, a goal for your outreach coordinator might be: "Increase parish participation in community service projects by 20% over the next six months, with a focus on engaging youth and promoting Catholic social teaching."

Performance management in a parish is not about creating a corporate culture but about helping each team member see their work as a vocation, a way to live out their faith in service to others.

Leading with Professional and Pastoral Care

As you implement these strategies, keep in mind the words of St. Paul: "We work with you for your joy" (2 Corinthians 1:24). Your role is not to be a taskmaster but a fellow laborer in Christ's vineyard, working alongside your team to bring joy and growth to your parish community.

By approaching performance management with this blend of professional rigor and pastoral care, you create an environment where your team can thrive, your parish can flourish, and together, you can more effectively build the Kingdom of God.

Managing Employees, Contractors, Virtual Assistants, and Volunteers: Similarities and Differences

Managing a parish team requires you to lead a diverse group of individuals, each with their own set of roles, expectations, and motivations. As a pastor, you'll often find yourself working with full-time employees, part-time contractors, virtual assistants (sometimes offshore), and volunteers. While these groups share certain similarities—such as the need for clear communication and a focus on the parish's mission—there are distinct differences in how you manage each. Understanding these differences is key to ensuring that all team members are motivated, productive, and aligned with the parish's goals.

Managing Employees: Commitment and Accountability

Employees are typically the core of your operational team, at least in most parishes in the U.S. and Canada. They are hired under formal employment agreements and work regular hours, with clear roles and responsibilities outlined in their job descriptions. Employees are expected to be fully committed to the parish's mission and goals, and they are usually compensated with a salary or hourly wages, as well as benefits (where applicable).

Key elements of managing employees:

- ▸ Clear Expectations: Employees require well-defined job descriptions that outline day-to-day tasks and long-term goals. Their role is often broader and more integrated into the parish's ongoing needs.

- ▸ Performance Management: Employees are subject to regular performance reviews, formal feedback sessions, and ongoing professional development. You need to provide clear pathways for growth, whether through training, mentorship, or increased responsibilities.

- ▸ Accountability: As employees are paid for their work, there is an inherent expectation of accountability. Poor performance, lack of effort, or failure to meet objectives should be addressed promptly through structured performance management.

- ▸ Cultural Alignment: Since employees spend more time engaged in parish work, they play a key role in shaping and maintaining the parish's culture. Ensuring that they align with the parish's values and mission is critical.

Employees typically have the highest level of involvement in the parish's operations, so it's important that they not only meet performance expectations but also represent the values of the Church in their day-to-day work.

Managing Contractors: Deliverables and Independence

Contractors are brought in to complete specific tasks or projects. They are not formal employees of the parish, and they often work on a contractual basis for a set period of time or until a specific deliverable is achieved. While contractors may have expertise in areas such as construction, IT, or marketing, they operate more independently and don't require the same level of oversight as employees.

Key elements of managing contractors:

▸ **Deliverables Focus:** Contractors are hired for specific projects or tasks, and success is measured based on the completion of these deliverables rather than ongoing responsibilities. The expectations must be crystal clear in terms of what is needed and when it is expected.

▸ **Independence:** Unlike employees, contractors are generally self-directed. They manage their own time, and as long as they meet their deadlines and deliver the required results, they have a degree of flexibility in how they work.

▸ **Limited Cultural Integration:** Contractors typically have less direct involvement in the day-to-day culture of the parish. While it's important that their work aligns with the parish's values, they aren't expected to engage in the broader life of the parish in the same way that employees are.

▸ **Temporary Engagement:** Since contractors are often brought in for specific tasks, their relationship with the parish is time-bound. Your management of them should focus on clear, results-oriented communications and regular check-ins on project progress.

When working with contractors, it's essential to ensure that their work contributes to the parish's overall mission, but you shouldn't need to manage them as closely as employees. A well-defined contract with clear deliverables and timelines is key to a successful partnership, along with regular communication

Managing Virtual Assistants (Offshore or Domestic) Communication and Clarity

Virtual assistants (VAs)—whether based domestically or offshore—provide remote support, often for administrative tasks, communications, or project management. Managing a virtual assistant requires you to be highly structured in communication and task assignment, as they are often not physically present in the parish office.

Key elements of managing virtual assistants:

▸ **Structured Communication:** Virtual assistants rely heavily on clear, concise instructions and consistent communication. Since they don't work in the physical office, you need to establish regular check-ins (via video calls, emails, or messaging apps) to ensure alignment.

▸ **Task-Specific Management:** VAs often perform specific, repeatable tasks such as data entry, scheduling, or responding to emails. They thrive when given well-defined tasks with specific instructions. They may not need to understand the broader context of parish operations but must know exactly what needs to be done.

▸ **Accountability Systems:** Since VAs work remotely, it's important to set up systems that track their progress, such as project management tools, shared calendars, or detailed task lists. They need clear deadlines and deliverables.

▸ **Cultural Alignment:** Offshore VAs, in particular, may not be as familiar with the nuances of your parish's culture or mission, so it's important to educate them on how their work supports the overall goals of the parish. While they may not be fully immersed in parish life, providing some context for their tasks helps them understand how their role fits into the bigger picture.

When managing virtual assistants, effective communication is crucial. Since they are working remotely, the focus should be on providing clear tasks, setting expectations, and creating a system of accountability that ensures they are meeting your needs.

Managing Volunteers: Motivation and Mission Alignment

Volunteers are a unique and vital part of the parish team. They serve out of a sense of mission and commitment to the Church, not for financial compensation. Managing volunteers requires a more pastoral approach, as their motivations are rooted in service and community rather than monetary reward

Key elements of managing volunteers:

▸▸ **Intrinsic Motivation:** Volunteers are driven by their faith and a desire to serve the parish. Your role as a pastor is to nurture this motivation, providing them with meaningful tasks that align with their sense of purpose and the parish's mission.

▸▸ **Flexible Expectations:** Unlike employees or contractors, volunteers have other commitments and are donating their time. This means that while clear expectations are important, you must also be flexible in how you manage their time and availability. Volunteers are more likely to stay engaged when they feel appreciated and when their contributions are valued.

▸▸ **Training and Support:** Volunteers may not have the same level of experience or skill as paid staff, so providing proper training and guidance is essential. Ongoing support ensures that they feel confident in their roles and continue to contribute meaningfully to parish life.

▸▸ **Recognition and Appreciation:** Since volunteers aren't compensated financially, recognition is key to keeping them motivated. Acknowledging their contributions during staff meetings, in the parish bulletin, or through personal notes goes a long way in fostering their continued involvement. Keep in mind that different people like to be recognized in different ways, sometimes publicly and sometimes not.

Managing volunteers requires a different approach from managing paid staff or contractors, yet they typically need more assistance, not less. Volunteers need to feel connected to the mission of the parish and should be continually encouraged, supported, and appreciated. A strong sense of community and recognition will keep them engaged and committed to their service.

While there are similarities in managing employees, contractors, virtual assistants, and volunteers—such as the need for clear communication and alignment with the parish's mission—the differences are crucial.

By tailoring your management approach to each of these groups, you can create a harmonious and productive team, each playing their part in fulfilling the parish's mission and building a thriving community of faith.

05

Meeting People Where They Are

The Diverse Paths to Faith

Why would we talk about something that is at the heart of the pastoral mission of the Church in a book about the business office? Pastors .are often frustrated that parishioners won't commit, won't sign up, or just don't seem interested. They are "consumers" rather than convicted, convinced, giving Catholics. This is true, but why? The reason is because each person is at different points in their faith journey. As St. Paul wrote, "I fed you milk, not solid food, because you were unable to take it. Indeed, you are still not able, even now, for you are still of the flesh." 1 Corinthians 3:2-23 Paul sees it as his job to give the community he founded truly nutritious food but in a state that they are able to consume so that they can grow and mature in their faith. Mother's milk and a steak are both nutritious, but milk is appropriate for an infant and a steak is not. That is still the job of the Church today.

Some might object that the reason the parish exists is to provide the sacraments, with the implication that people just have to take it or leave it. While the sacraments are the primary means to grace, and therefore essential to the mission of the Church, they are a means to an end, not the end in themselves. They should be the main stepping stones along our faith journey, but it is the final destination that we seek, which is God himself. A God that many "sacramentalized" Catholics do not know personally. If we truly want to baptize all nations, we have to win individual minds and hearts for Jesus, so we have to know where those hearts are and speak to them. If we design an amazingly efficient business office machine, but lose sight of this key part of our mission, we haven't done anyone a service.

The Spectrum of Belonging

Don't think of "belonging" as a binary yes/no answer but as a spectrum. On one end, you have low belonging and low commitment. On the other, you have total belonging and total commitment. In between is a sliding scale along that continuum.

While we won't get into strategies to increase the sense of belonging in this book, we do want to talk about the different places people can be spiritually, because ultimately it is the personal relationship with God that keeps people from slipping backwards. Understanding this spectrum can help you navigate the complex landscape of parish alignment. It allows you to meet people where they are while also providing opportunities for deeper faith and commitment. Why do they come to Mass, ask to baptize their children, or send their children to a Catholic school? Each person has their own reasons, but here are some common answers.

In a world often fraught with moral ambiguities, the church offers a clear moral and ethical framework. People are drawn to its teachings that provide a foundation for leading a life of virtue and purpose, offering a compass for navigating the complexities of ethical living.

The sacred rituals and sacraments also draw many. These time-honored traditions mark significant life milestones and provide regular spiritual sustenance, anchoring individuals in a rhythm of faith that nourishes and sustains them.

There are those who come seeking the beauty and richness of Church culture, its art, music, and architecture. They find inspiration and awe in the Church's ability to capture the divine through human creativity and expression.

Service and outreach are other powerful magnets that draw people. Driven by a desire to make a difference and serve others, individuals find fulfillment in the Church's commitment to charity, social justice, and community service.

Personal healing and transformation also guide many. Seeking solace, healing, or a new beginning, they turn to the Church as a source of hope, strength, and Renewal.

Educational opportunities offered by the Church attract those eager to deepen their understanding of faith, Scripture, and ethics. The Church becomes a classroom for the mind and spirit, where learning and growth go hand in hand.

There are other common reasons people come to the Catholic Church, which are usually implicit and not stated. Sometimes people might not even be aware of them, but they are very real. One reason some people come to Church is for cultural or social pressure. Many pastors have experienced couples who want to get married in the Church more because a grandparent wants them to. Often people will enroll their children in Catholic schools because they believe there will be a better education or less bullying, and so forth.

As each person walks their path within the Church, their reasons for being there may shift, deepen, or transform, reflecting the dynamic nature of faith and life. The Church, in her wisdom, offers a multitude of ways to meet individuals where they are, accompanying them on their journey with a tapestry of experiences

and opportunities tailored to their evolving needs and aspirations. All of these motivations are hopefully on-ramps for them into the journey of faith towards God through the Church. "Through the Church" implies that there is a community of people. Every human person wants to be fully known and loved and respected as they are. So for evangelization to occur, we need to have a healthy community first, much like you cannot paint a beautiful scene without the canvas.

This diversity of paths is beautifully exemplified in the story of Fr. John, a newly ordained priest excited to learn the intricacies of celebrating sacraments. Initially, he felt a sense of accomplishment in mastering the rituals and managing the crowds. However, over time, he started to notice that his parishioners seemed to be going through the motions without truly converting. They were more concerned about homilies that made them feel good rather than ones that challenged them, and approached the sacraments as mere formalities rather than as opportunities to deepen their relationship with God. Fr. John's experience highlights the importance of recognizing and addressing the various stages of faith development within a parish community. Without this understanding, parish work and ministry can be very frustrating

Statistics underscore the urgency of engaging individuals at different points in their faith journey. According to a 2014 study by the Pew Research Center, 77% of Catholics who leave the Church do so before the age of twenty-four. This staggering figure emphasizes the critical need for parishes to provide relevant, engaging, and meaningful experiences for young people, while also being sure to engage parents in the process, since without parents living out the faith there is little possibility of success for the children.

The challenge for pastors and parish leaders lies in understanding and appreciating these diverse entry points and motivations. As President Theodore Roosevelt once said, "People don't care how much you know until they know how much you care." This sentiment rings particularly true in the context of parish life. To effectively shepherd their flock, pastors must first demonstrate genuine care, empathy, and understanding for each individual's unique journey.

The Cradle Catholic, the Convert, and the One Who Left and Returned

Within the tapestry of a Church community, there are three general categories that we can start to understand before we get into more specific situations. These three distinct stories are the cradle Catholic, the convert, and the one who left and returned, sometimes called the "revert." Each narrative is a unique thread woven into the larger fabric of faith and spirituality.

The cradle Catholic, born into the faith, is like a well-rooted tree, firmly established in the traditions, rituals, and teachings from an early age. Their journey of faith often begins in infancy, marked by sacraments like baptism and confirmation. They grow up attending Mass, receiving the Eucharist, and participating in religious education. For the cradle Catholic, the Church is an integral part of their identity and upbringing, providing a sense of continuity and a deep-rooted connection to tradition. Yet, their faith journey is not without its challenges. They may grapple with questions and doubts along the way, seeking to truly understand and internalize the faith they've inherited.

The convert, on the other hand, embarks on a path of deliberate choice and discovery. They come as seekers, driven by a quest for truth, meaning, and spiritual fulfillment. The journey of the convert often involves a profound awakening or a series of transformative experiences that lead them to embrace the Catholic faith. It is a path marked by personal exploration, inquiry, and often, a conscious decision to convert to Catholicism. The convert's faith is not inherited but chosen, making their commitment to the Church a testament to their genuine conviction and deepening relationship with God. Their unique perspective often brings fresh insights and enthusiasm to the faith community.

The one who left and returned has a story of departure and homecoming, marked by a period of distance. At some point, they drifted away, disillusioned or disheartened by personal struggles, doubts, or external influences. Their absence may span months, years, or even decades. Yet, something within them calls them back—a longing for the spiritual home they once knew or a yearning for the sense of purpose and belonging they once found in the Church. The journey of return is often accompanied by a sense of humility, reconciliation, and a profound encounter with God's mercy. The one who left and returned brings the gift of renewed faith and a powerful testimony of God's love and forgiveness to the community.

These three individuals represent the diverse paths of faith that converge within the Church. While their stories may differ in origin and trajectory, they all share a common thread—the desire to seek, find, and deepen their relationship with God. Within the community of faith, each person's narrative enriches the collective tapestry, reminding us that faith is a dynamic and deeply personal journey, marked by unique experiences, challenges, and revelations. Together, they form a vibrant mosaic of faith, reflecting the multifaceted nature of the human spirit's quest for transcendence and connection with the divine.

The Atheist and Agnostic

We will now describe the various types of people as regards their faith life starting with the far extreme, atheists and agnostics. While there are probably few of these in most common parish settings, it is important to keep them in mind when it comes to outreach efforts, weddings and funerals, or other moments when there are many non-parishioners present such as Christmas and Easter Masses.

Atheists and agnostics represent a diverse group of individuals, many of whom may have encountered faith but have, for various reasons, chosen to distance themselves from belief in God or remain uncertain about His existence. Atheists do not believe in the existence of God, while agnostics hold that the existence of God is either uncertain or unknowable. Their worldviews often prioritize secular, humanistic, or scientific perspectives, placing a high value on empirical evidence, rational thought, and personal autonomy.

It's important to remember that people become atheists or agnostics for any number of reasons—some of which they may be aware of, and others they may not fully understand. There may be intellectual barriers, emotional wounds, or negative experiences with religious institutions that contribute to their stance. As followers of Christ, we are called to engage these individuals with love, understanding, and patience, always remembering that faith is a journey, and God works in people's hearts in ways we may not immediately see.

Atheism and agnosticism cut across many demographic lines, though certain trends have emerged. Younger adults are more likely to identify with these perspectives, especially in highly secularized societies. Education plays a significant role as well, with many atheists and agnostics having high levels of academic achievement, particularly in fields that encourage critical thinking and skepticism, such as science, philosophy, and the humanities. Despite these trends, atheism and agnosticism are present in every culture and demographic.

Atheists and agnostics often place great importance on values such as personal autonomy, logical reasoning, and the pursuit of knowledge through evidence. For many, the search for meaning is tied to what can be known and proven through reason, experience, and the senses. This does not mean they lack a sense of wonder or morality; rather, they are motivated by the desire to understand the world through a framework that excludes what they cannot empirically verify.

That said, their motivations are not always purely intellectual. Some may be seeking healing from past negative experiences with religious communities, while others may simply feel disconnected from the idea of God due to life circumstances that are hard to reconcile with faith. It's crucial to approach such individuals with empathy, understanding that their journey may be complex and personal.

In terms of information consumption and communication, atheists and agnostics are often drawn to secular and scientific media. They tend to engage with publications, websites, and forums that promote rational thought, critical analysis, and skepticism. They may follow prominent figures in science, philosophy, or secular ethics, and they generally prefer clear, reasoned arguments over emotional or faith-based appeals.

When engaging in dialogue, it's important to recognize that many atheists and agnostics will approach conversations with a natural skepticism. They are often wary of claims that lack empirical evidence and may view religious language with suspicion. Therefore, conversations grounded in mutual respect, clear reasoning, and genuine curiosity tend to be more productive.

Despite differing beliefs, there are several meaningful ways to engage atheists and agnostics. Many of these individuals are deeply committed to causes such as social justice, community service, and intellectual exploration. These shared values offer points of connection:

▸ Community events that focus on helping the vulnerable or addressing social issues can create common ground for collaboration.

- Intellectual forums where ethics, philosophy, and science are discussed in a respectful and thoughtful manner often appeal to their desire for deeper understanding.

- Personal relationships with Christians who demonstrate authentic respect, humility, and curiosity about their worldview can open doors to more profound spiritual discussions.

Engaging atheists and agnostics is not without its challenges. Many approach religious claims with skepticism, particularly those that seem to conflict with their understanding of reason or science. Misconceptions about the Church—such as the idea that faith and reason are incompatible—can further hinder dialogue.

Additionally, some individuals may have had negative experiences with religious institutions. These experiences, which may have involved judgmental attitudes or perceived anti-intellectualism, can leave emotional scars. It's important to recognize and address these concerns with compassion, acknowledging where the Church has fallen short and where misunderstandings have occurred.

When speaking with atheists and agnostics, it's important to use language that fosters respect, openness, and curiosity. Some approaches that work well include:

- Genuine Curiosity: "I'd love to hear more about your experiences and how they've shaped your perspective on spirituality."

- Respect for Beliefs: "I can see that you value logical reasoning and evidence. I respect how thoughtfully you've formed your views."

- Personal Experience Sharing: "My faith has provided comfort and guidance through tough times. Have you ever had experiences that made you reflect on life's deeper questions?"

- Open Dialogue: "I'd really appreciate having a conversation where we can both share and learn from each other's perspectives. I think we can both grow through these discussions."

- Inclusive Language: "In our community, we have people from a variety of beliefs, and these different viewpoints make for rich, meaningful dialogue."

- Insightful Sharing: "For me, faith has been less about doctrine and more about a relationship with God. Everyone's journey looks different, and that's okay."

▸ Understanding Skepticism: "I completely understand why you're skeptical about religious claims. It's important to question and seek truth."

▸ Empathy and Compassion: "I appreciate your honesty. These conversations can be difficult, but understanding each other better is always worthwhile."

▸ Encouraging Exploration: "Life is a journey, and our beliefs evolve over time. Whether it's through philosophy, science, or faith, there's always something new to explore."

▸ Inviting Further Conversation: "I've enjoyed this conversation. Maybe we could continue it over coffee or at an event sometime. I think these discussions are valuable."

Engaging atheists and agnostics requires patience, empathy, and a deep understanding of their perspectives. By approaching them with humility, respect for their values, and a willingness to listen, meaningful dialogue can emerge. The reasons someone may identify as an atheist or agnostic are varied and personal, and as Catholics, our role is not to convince but to witness—to be a living example of Christ's love, truth, and mercy. Over time, through relationships, service, and thoughtful conversations, these interactions may open hearts to the possibility of faith, but it must always be done with love and respect for the journey each individual is on.

Cultural Catholic

The "Cultural Catholic" group consists of individuals who identify as Catholic primarily due to cultural heritage, family tradition, or social ties, often attending Mass only on significant holidays like Christmas and Easter. While they may have been baptized as infants or married into a Catholic family, their connection to the faith is often more cultural than deeply spiritual, lacking a robust personal conversion of the heart. These individuals participate in Church life out of a sense of obligation, respect for tradition, or for social reasons, rather than a profound desire for spiritual growth or active engagement with Catholic teachings. They may view the Church as a significant part of their personal or family history but not necessarily as a guiding force in their daily lives.

The worldview of the Cultural Catholic is shaped by tradition, family, and a sense of belonging to a historical community rather than an active, personal faith journey. Their understanding of Catholicism is often limited to cultural practices and major holidays.

Definition: Individuals who identify as Catholic primarily through cultural, familial, or social ties, typically attending Mass only on Christmas and Easter, without a strong personal spiritual conviction.

Worldview: A sense of belonging to a cultural heritage, viewing Catholicism as a tradition or a familial obligation, rather than a deeply personal or active faith.

Their perspective on spirituality is often passive or intermittent. They may see it as a cultural custom to be observed on specific occasions, rather than an ongoing relationship with God or a daily practice. They might respect religious rituals but do not necessarily feel personally connected to their deeper meaning.

Cultural Catholics often value family unity, heritage, and the social aspects of community. Their motivations are typically driven by a desire to uphold family traditions, fulfill social expectations, or maintain a connection to their roots.

Values: Family tradition, cultural identity, community cohesion, and respect for heritage.

Motivations: Fulfilling familial expectations, maintaining social ties, honoring cultural heritage, and participating in significant family or community events.

Cultural Catholics are unlikely to actively seek out religious content. When they do engage, it might be through general media that touches upon holiday themes or cultural celebrations. They prefer communication that is non-intrusive, welcoming, and focuses on community and shared experiences.

 Media Consumption: Minimal engagement with specific religious content, possibly some exposure to general media related to holidays (e.g., Christmas specials, Easter narratives).

Communication Styles: Prefer welcoming, respectful, and low-pressure communication that emphasizes community and shared heritage rather than theological depth or personal spiritual challenge.

There are opportunities to engage with this group by highlighting the Church's role in family life, cultural celebrations, and community building, without imposing heavy spiritual demands. Invitations should be gentle and focus on fostering a sense of belonging.

Family-Oriented Events: Invite them to events that are culturally significant or appeal to families, such as parish festivals, holiday pageants, or community service initiatives.

Welcoming and Low-Pressure Interactions: Provide opportunities for casual interaction that don't immediately require deep spiritual commitment, focusing on fellowship and a sense of shared community.

Despite their strong cultural ties, Cultural Catholics may face challenges in reconciling their identity with the Church's call for active faith and personal commitment. They may also feel a disconnect between their traditional practices and the evolving dynamics of parish life.

Lack of Personal Connection: The absence of a personal spiritual conviction can make deeper engagement feel inauthentic or unfulfilling.

Perception of Irrelevance: They might perceive the Church's teachings or activities as disconnected from their daily lives or as overly demanding.

Effective communication with Cultural Catholics should be welcoming and non-judgmental, emphasizing the Church as a place of belonging, community, and support for families. Messages should highlight the enduring value of Catholic traditions and the communal aspects of faith.

Emphasizing Community and Heritage: Focus on the Church as a place where family traditions are honored and community bonds are strengthened.

Gentle Invitation to Deeper Engagement: Offer soft invitations to explore more about the faith, framing it as an opportunity for personal enrichment or deeper connection to heritage, rather than an obligation.

When communicating with Cultural Catholics, it's important to use language that affirms their presence and respects their cultural ties, while gently inviting them to consider a deeper connection to the faith.

Acknowledgement and Welcome: "It's wonderful to see you here, especially during these special times of year. Your presence enriches our parish community."

Invitation to Community: "Our parish offers many ways for families to connect and celebrate throughout the year, beyond just the holidays. We invite you to explore them!"

Highlighting Heritage: "The Catholic faith is rich with traditions that have sustained families for generations. We're here to help you explore and deepen your connection to this beautiful heritage."

Non-Catholic Parents of Catholic School Children

The "Non-Catholic Parents of Catholic School Children" group comprises individuals who have chosen to enroll their children in a Catholic school despite not being Catholic themselves. Their primary motivation often stems from the school's reputation for academic excellence, strong moral values, discipline, safety, or a nurturing community environment. While they appreciate the values-based education their children receive, their own personal faith may vary widely—from other Christian denominations or other religions to agnosticism or atheism. Their interaction with the Church is primarily through the school, attending school events, parent-teacher conferences, school Masses (often as observers), and supporting school-related activities. They seek a high-quality educational experience for their children, with a respectful understanding that religious instruction is part of the curriculum.

The worldview of these parents is centered on their children's well-being and future success, seeing Catholic schools as providing a beneficial environment for academic, moral, and social development. They may hold a general respect for faith and values, even if they don't personally adhere to Catholic doctrine.

Definition: Parents who are not Catholic but choose to send their children to Catholic schools, often prioritizing academic quality, moral formation, and community environment for their children.

Worldview: Focused on providing the best educational and developmental environment for their children, appreciating the values and discipline offered by Catholic schools, often with a general respect for faith, though not necessarily sharing Catholic beliefs themselves.

Their perspective on spirituality is largely practical, viewing it as a component of their child's holistic education, contributing to character formation and moral grounding. For themselves, spirituality may be expressed through their own faith tradition, or it may not be a central part of their lives; they typically do not seek personal spiritual growth within the Catholic Church context for themselves.

Non-Catholic parents highly value quality education, strong moral and ethical formation for their children, a safe and disciplined environment, and a supportive community. Their motivations are driven by a desire for their children to excel academically, develop strong character, and be part of a positive peer group.

Values: Academic excellence, strong moral and ethical development for their children, a disciplined and safe learning environment, and a supportive school community.

Motivations: Providing their children with a high-quality education, character formation, positive social development, and a values-rich upbringing.

These parents primarily consume media related to parenting, education, and general news. They are unlikely to actively seek out Catholic theological content unless it directly pertains to their child's school curriculum or specific school events. They prefer clear, direct, and inclusive communication.

Media Consumption: Engage with school communications (newsletters, emails, websites), educational resources, and general news. Less likely to seek specific Catholic media unless directly relevant to school activities.

Communication Styles: Prefer clear, practical, and respectful communication. Appreciate transparency regarding school expectations, academic progress, and how religious instruction is integrated. They respond well to inclusive language that emphasizes shared goals for their children's success.

There are numerous opportunities to engage with this group through school-based activities and broader parish initiatives that demonstrate support for the school

community. Creating spaces where they feel welcome and respected, regardless of their faith background, is key.

School Community Events: Invite them to school-sponsored social events, fundraisers, parent volunteer opportunities, and academic showcases that foster a sense of belonging within the school community.

Informational Sessions: Offer optional, low-pressure sessions that explain aspects of Catholic faith or traditions relevant to the school curriculum, emphasizing how these contribute to character development.

Despite their positive engagement with Catholic schools, these parents may encounter challenges related to feeling like outsiders in a predominantly Catholic environment. They might also grapple with how to discuss or explain Catholic teachings to their children when they don't share the faith themselves.

Navigating Religious Curriculum: Uncertainty about how to best support their children's religious education without personally adhering to the faith.

Feeling Like Outsiders: May occasionally feel a disconnect or "othered" in deeply religious school or parish contexts, particularly during overtly Catholic celebrations or liturgical events.

Effective communication to this group should emphasize the shared mission of nurturing children's growth—academically, morally, and spiritually—within the school environment. Highlighting the school's commitment to all families, regardless of faith, and offering resources to understand the Catholic dimension without pressure are crucial.

Emphasizing Shared Mission: Focus on the common goals of educating and forming well-rounded children, highlighting how the school's values align with their parental aspirations.

Inclusive and Resource-Oriented Content: Provide clear information about how faith is integrated into the curriculum, offering resources for parents to understand (without expectation of conversion) and support their children's learning journey.

When communicating with non-Catholic parents of Catholic school children, it's important to use language that affirms their choice of Catholic education and acknowledges their vital role in the school community, while respecting their personal faith journey.

Appreciation for Their Choice: "Thank you for entrusting your child's education to our Catholic school. We are committed to providing an exceptional learning environment for every student."

Invitation to School Community: "Your involvement is a vital part of our school community. We invite you to participate in school events and volunteer opportunities, helping to make our school thrive."

Shared Values of Education: "We share your commitment to nurturing your child's academic potential and character development, grounded in the values that guide our Catholic education."

If they wish for their children to receive the sacraments, or the children ask to receive them, it opens up the possibility for a deeper conversation about faith and the gap between how they want their children to grow up and the faith in their home today.

The Curious

The "Spiritual but Not Religious" group or curious seekers includes individuals who believe in some form of spirituality or higher power but do not align themselves with organized religion or specific religious doctrines. They might come to your parish with friends, to attend an event, or just out of curiosity. These individuals often believe in the interconnectedness of life or a greater universal spirit but feel that formalized religious structures do not resonate with their personal spiritual journey. Their worldview tends to be holistic, emphasizing personal growth, mindfulness, and inner peace over adherence to dogma. Practices such as meditation, yoga, or spiritual rituals that promote self-reflection are common, as they seek to nurture their spiritual life outside traditional religious frameworks.

This group spans a wide age range but is especially prevalent among millennials and Gen Z, who are often exploring alternative spiritual paths. Many within this demographic are well-educated, open to new ideas, and culturally diverse. Their spiritual curiosity leads them to explore different practices and perspectives, yet they often avoid rigid systems of belief. Rather than subscribing to a single religious

tradition, they seek inspiration from various sources, adapting and integrating spiritual practices that resonate with their personal experiences and values.

At the heart of this group's values is an emphasis on personal spiritual experience, self-discovery, authenticity, and a desire for connection to a greater whole. They are motivated by the quest for inner peace, the pursuit of understanding the self and the universe, and a desire to live harmoniously within the world. Their spirituality is often deeply personal, tied to their own experiences and reflections, rather than external religious authority. This focus on individual experience makes them wary of systems that prescribe a fixed spiritual path.

In terms of behaviors and preferences, the "Spiritual but Not Religious" group is likely to engage with content centered around personal development, wellness, and spirituality outside of traditional religious institutions. They are drawn to media that explores mindfulness, environmentalism, and personal well-being. Digital platforms that offer meditative practices, holistic health advice, or discussions on spiritual exploration resonate deeply with them. They prefer communication that is open, inclusive, and non-dogmatic, valuing conversations that acknowledge multiple spiritual paths rather than a singular truth.

Engagement opportunities with this group can be found in community events focused on spirituality, healing, and social justice. Retreats that focus on spirituality, meditation, or personal growth often attract their attention, as do events that promote environmental stewardship and social justice causes. Ecumenical and interfaith activities, where multiple spiritual traditions are discussed in a non-prescriptive manner, also appeal to their exploratory nature. They are often open to dialogue around spirituality, as long as it is presented in a way that respects their individuality and avoids the rigidity they may associate with organized religion.

However, there are potential barriers to engagement. Many in this group hold reservations or negative past experiences with organized religion, viewing it as overly institutionalized or dogmatic. This can make them hesitant to engage with religious communities, particularly if they perceive that community as trying to impose a specific belief system. Their spirituality is often fluid and individualistic, making one-size-fits-all approaches ineffective. Approaching them with a genuine respect for their spiritual autonomy and a willingness to meet them where they are is essential for meaningful dialogue.

To engage effectively, communication strategies should focus on inclusive messaging that highlights the universal aspects of spirituality present within Catholic teachings, such as love, peace, and community. Emphasizing the Church's commitment to personal growth, social justice, and environmental care can resonate with their values. Highlighting Catholic teachings that promote personal development, contemplation, and a sense of connection with the broader world will create opportunities to introduce them to the faith in a way that feels both inclusive and relevant.

When communicating with the "Spiritual but Not Religious" group, it's important to use open, welcoming language that respects their spiritual journey. For example, open-ended invitations like, "We'd love for you to join our community discussion on spirituality and its role in modern life. We're exploring various perspectives and would greatly value yours," can help create an inviting space. Acknowledging diversity is also crucial: "Our faith community recognizes and respects the many paths people take in their spiritual journey. Let's share and learn from our different experiences." Additionally, it helps to emphasize the personal journey: "In our parish, we believe in supporting each individual's spiritual journey. You might find our meditation group and silent retreats particularly enriching."

This profile acknowledges the unique nature of the "Spiritual but Not Religious" group, offering insights into how to connect with them in a respectful and effective manner. By recognizing their quest for personal spirituality and introducing them to the Catholic community in a way that honors their individual experiences, there is potential for meaningful engagement and exploration of the Catholic faith within the context of their broader spiritual search.

Beginner in Faith

The "Beginner in Faith" group consists of individuals who have recently discovered or developed an interest in the Catholic faith and are taking their first steps toward understanding and practicing it. Often, they are at the start of their spiritual journey, whether through the Order of Christian Initiation of Adults (OCIA) or other introductory catechetical programs. These individuals are curious, eager to learn, and seeking a sense of belonging in the Catholic community as they begin to explore the rich teachings and traditions of the Church.

These individuals are open to new spiritual insights and practices, as they have recently found belief in God and are exploring the Catholic faith. Their worldview is one of openness and discovery as they seek guidance and answers to spiritual questions.

- ⏩ **Definition:** Recently begun their faith journey, exploring Catholicism and seeking a deeper understanding of the faith.
- ⏩ **Worldview:** Open to learning, spiritually curious, and eager to find a sense of community and purpose within the Church.

They often enter this journey with enthusiasm but may also feel uncertain or overwhelmed by the depth of the Catholic tradition. Many are motivated by a desire for spiritual growth, truth, and a connection with God that is both personal and communal.

- ⏩ **Values**: Curiosity, openness to learning, desire for spiritual growth and a supportive community.
- ⏩ **Motivations**: Want to understand Catholic teachings, grow closer to God, and connect with a faith-based community that can nurture their spiritual journey.

This group is looking for guidance and reassurance as they navigate their newfound faith, often feeling a mixture of excitement and uncertainty as they explore Catholic practices and teachings.

Those in the "Beginner in Faith" group typically consume beginner-level religious content as they build a foundation for their faith. They appreciate clear, straightforward communication that nurtures their curiosity and addresses their questions without overwhelming them. They thrive in environments where they can explore their faith at a comfortable pace and receive support from more experienced parishioners.

- ⏩ **Media Consumption**: Likely to engage with introductory books on Catholicism, basic theology resources, and accessible spiritual writings.
- ⏩ **Communication Styles:** Prefer clear, straightforward, and nurturing communication. Appreciate the ability to ask questions and express doubts without fear of judgment.

They are also drawn to content that helps explain Catholic practices, prayers, and rituals in an accessible and approachable manner.

There are numerous ways to engage this group, particularly through educational programs and parish activities designed to help them grow in their understanding of the faith and integrate into the community.

▸▸ **Educational Programs:** Interested in OCIA, catechism classes, and other introductory religious education offerings that provide a strong foundation in Catholic teachings.

▸▸ **Parish Activities:** Likely to engage in Bible study groups, social gatherings, and other parish events that help them feel welcomed and part of the faith community.

This group benefits from structured, yet welcoming, programs that give them the tools they need to grow in their faith while also providing the social support that helps them feel connected to the parish.

As excited as they are to begin their journey, "Beginners in Faith" may face some challenges, such as feeling overwhelmed by the vastness of Catholic teachings or finding it difficult to adapt to a new community. It's important to help them navigate these potential obstacles with care and understanding.

Providing clear, gradual instruction and fostering a welcoming atmosphere can ease these concerns, helping them feel more confident and comfortable in their faith journey.

Effective communication to this group involves providing content that is welcoming, educational, and tailored to the needs of newcomers. Offering resources that explain Catholic practices and provide answers to common questions is key, as is highlighting the supportive, family-like nature of the parish.

▸▸ **Welcoming and Educational Content:** Provide accessible resources for beginners, explaining Catholic beliefs and practices in a simple, clear way.

▸▸ **Mentorship Programs:** Pair beginners with more experienced parishioners who can offer guidance and support as they navigate their new faith journey.

▸ **Highlighting Community Aspects:** Showcase the parish's welcoming and supportive community, emphasizing the role of fellowship and spiritual growth.

By offering a clear path for learning and integrating into the Church community, you can make the parish feel like a place where beginners can grow both spiritually and socially.

When speaking with beginners in the faith, it's important to use encouraging, supportive language that fosters a sense of belonging and openness to learning. Language that affirms their decision to explore the faith and reassures them that they are supported in their journey can make a significant impact.

▸ **Encouraging and Supportive:** "We're so glad you're exploring your faith with us. We're here to support you every step of the way and answer any questions you might have."

▸ **Inviting to Learn:** "Our parish offers various programs that are perfect for those new to the faith. They're a great way to learn more in a friendly, welcoming environment."

▸ **Fostering Belonging:** "You're now a part of our church family, and we're excited to walk this journey of faith alongside you."

These messages create an environment of welcome and reassurance, ensuring that beginners feel confident and comfortable as they take their first steps in the Catholic faith.

Newly Baptized / Converted

The "Newly Baptized/Converted" group consists of individuals who have recently joined the Catholic Church through either baptism or conversion. These individuals are at the beginning of their Christian life and are often filled with enthusiasm, a desire to learn, and a sense of wonder about their newfound faith. They seek to integrate Catholic beliefs, practices, and teachings into their daily lives, and many are eager to become active participants in the Church community. While they are motivated by a fresh commitment to the Church, they may also face challenges as they adjust to their new spiritual and social environment.

The worldview of the newly baptized or converted is one of fresh spiritual awakening. They are deeply committed to learning about their new faith and practicing Catholic teachings, often filled with a sense of excitement and devotion as they begin their journey.

- ▸▸ **Definition:** Recently baptized or converted individuals who have joined the Catholic Church and are in the early stages of their new Christian life.

- ▸▸ **Worldview:** A newfound commitment to Catholicism, coupled with enthusiasm and a desire to deepen their understanding of Catholic beliefs and practices.

Their perspective on spirituality has been transformed through their initiation into the Church, and they are often eager to grow closer to God by fully embracing the teachings and traditions of the Catholic faith.

Newly baptized and converted individuals often value spiritual growth, a sense of belonging, and the opportunity to live out their faith in practical ways. They are motivated to learn more about the Catholic faith and integrate it into every aspect of their lives, from participating in the sacraments to being active members of the parish community.

- ▸▸ **Values:** A desire for spiritual growth, a strong sense of community belonging, and commitment to living out their newfound faith.

- ▸▸ **Motivations:** Motivated to learn more about Catholic teachings, grow in their relationship with God, participate in the sacraments, and become integrated into the faith community.

They are eager to learn how their faith can transform their lives and how they can contribute to the life of the Church.

Newly baptized and converted individuals are likely to seek out content that helps them deepen their understanding of Catholic teachings and practices. They appreciate clear, supportive communication that encourages them in their new faith journey while providing practical guidance.

- ▸▸ **Media Consumption:** Engage with introductory religious content such as basic theology, explanations of Catholic practices, and spiritual guides for beginners.

▸ **Communication Styles:** Prefer nurturing, affirming, and clear communication, as they are often seeking reassurance and guidance as they navigate their new faith.

They may initially rely on resources like books, online courses, or discussions with more experienced Catholics to help them better understand Catholic doctrines and traditions.

There are numerous opportunities to engage with this group, particularly through follow-up programs designed to support their ongoing faith journey after baptism or conversion. Providing pathways for deeper learning and integration into the parish community can help them feel more confident in their new identity as Catholics.

▸ **Follow-up Programs:** Offer post-OCIA groups, catechetical classes, or other faith formation programs that support continued learning and spiritual growth.

▸ **Community Integration Activities:** Invite them to participate in parish life through small group meetings, social events, or volunteer opportunities that help them connect with others and feel like part of the community.

By providing spaces for continued learning and social integration, the Church can help these individuals deepen their faith and form lasting relationships with other parishioners.

Despite their enthusiasm, newly baptized and converted individuals may encounter challenges as they adjust to their new spiritual and social environment. It's important to provide support that helps them navigate these difficulties without feeling overwhelmed.

▸ **Adjusting to a New Faith Community:** Learning to navigate a new religious and social environment can feel intimidating or unfamiliar.

▸ **Overwhelm with Church Teachings:** The depth and breadth of Catholic doctrine may feel overwhelming at first, leading to uncertainty about where to start or how to prioritize learning.

Providing clear and structured guidance, as well as fostering a welcoming environment, can help mitigate these challenges and ensure that they feel supported.

Effective communication to this group should emphasize the welcoming and supportive nature of the Church while providing resources specifically tailored to their needs as new members. Highlighting the importance of community, mentorship, and continued learning can help them feel more confident and secure in their faith.

- ▸▸ **Welcoming and Guiding Content:** Provide resources such as welcome packets, introductory courses, and mentorship programs that are specifically designed for new members of the faith.
- ▸▸ **Emphasizing Community and Belonging:** Showcase the parish's commitment to welcoming newcomers and fostering a supportive community. Encourage involvement in church activities and events that emphasize fellowship and spiritual growth.

Highlighting the Church's openness and the community's eagerness to welcome new members is key to helping them feel fully integrated into their new faith.

When communicating with newly baptized or converted individuals, it's important to use language that affirms their decision to join the Church and offers ongoing support as they continue their spiritual journey.

- ▸▸ **Encouragement and Affirmation**: "Congratulations on taking this significant step in your faith journey! We are here to support and guide you as you grow in your new life in Christ."
- ▸▸ **Invitation to Learn and Grow:** "Our parish offers a variety of resources and programs to help you deepen your understanding and practice of the faith. We encourage you to explore and participate."
- ▸▸ **Building Community Connections:** "You are an important part of our church family. We invite you to join our community groups and events to connect with other members and build lasting relationships."

Using encouraging and affirming language helps build confidence and reinforces that they are now part of a supportive and welcoming community that values their presence.

Struggling Parishioners

The "Struggling Individual" group consists of individuals who are clearly facing difficulties in their faith journey, often due to personal challenges, scandals, or public sin. These individuals may feel alienated from the Church and community, burdened by guilt, shame, or a sense of unworthiness. They are in need of both pastoral care and compassionate guidance to help them navigate their struggles, reconcile with the Church, and find healing and renewal in their relationship with God. The Church's role is to offer them a path to repentance, healing, and reintegration into the community, following the example of Christ's mercy.

Struggling individuals often find themselves at a crossroads in their faith due to personal challenges or moral failings. While they may still believe in the core teachings of the Church, they often feel distant or disconnected due to the weight of their struggles.

- **Definition:** Individuals dealing with a personal scandal, public sin, or other significant challenges that have affected their spiritual and community life.

- **Worldview:** Their faith may be clouded by feelings of guilt, shame, or alienation. They may view themselves as unworthy or disconnected from the Church, often struggling to reconcile their actions with their beliefs.

While their worldview may have been shaped by the teachings of the Church, their current struggle often makes it difficult for them to live out their faith authentically.

Struggling individuals are often motivated by a desire to find peace, forgiveness, and reconciliation. Despite their challenges, they may still value faith, community, and spiritual growth, but they are often overwhelmed by their current situation.

- **Values:** May still hold deep values for faith, forgiveness, and redemption but feel distant from them due to their struggles.

- **Motivations:** Motivated by a desire for reconciliation, healing, and a return to spiritual wholeness, though they may not know how to seek these things.

Their motivation often hinges on their ability to believe that redemption is possible. The Church can play a critical role in helping them rediscover hope and healing.

Struggling individuals may withdraw from parish life, avoiding Mass or community events out of shame or fear of judgment. They may engage less with spiritual content, feeling unworthy or disconnected from the Church's message.

- ▶▶ **Media Consumption:** Likely to avoid typical religious content, focusing more on content that speaks to personal struggles, recovery, or self-help.
- ▶▶ **Communication Styles:** Prefer gentle, compassionate, and non-judgmental communication that offers understanding and hope. They may need time and space to open up and express their struggles.

They may struggle with trust and require careful pastoral outreach to help them feel comfortable and safe in sharing their challenges.

Pastoral care and the sacraments offer key opportunities for guiding struggling individuals back into the fold. They may benefit from confidential spiritual direction, reconciliation programs, and opportunities to reintegrate into the community through acts of service.

- ▶▶ **Spiritual Direction and Counseling:** Providing confidential, one-on-one guidance through spiritual direction, counseling, or sacramental reconciliation.
- ▶▶ **Reintegration into Parish Life:** Inviting them to participate in ministries focused on healing, such as grief counseling, support groups, or outreach to others facing challenges.

These opportunities help struggling individuals find their place in the Church again, offering them pathways for personal healing and spiritual growth.

Struggling individuals face significant internal and external barriers to reconciliation with the Church. They may feel overwhelmed by guilt or shame, fear judgment from others, or believe they are unworthy of forgiveness. These barriers can prevent them from seeking help and engaging with the Church community.

- ▶▶ **Shame and Guilt:** Feelings of deep shame and guilt may prevent them from approaching the Church or seeking help.

- ▸ **Fear of Judgment:** A fear of judgment from fellow parishioners or Church leaders may cause them to isolate themselves further from the community.

- ▸ **Despair:** They may feel that their sins or struggles are too great to be forgiven, leading to despair and a sense of hopelessness.

Pastoral leaders must approach them with mercy and patience, creating a safe and non-judgmental environment that invites them to return to the faith.

Reaching out to struggling individuals requires careful and sensitive messaging that emphasizes God's mercy, the Church's role in healing, and the unconditional love available through Christ. Programs focused on reconciliation, forgiveness, and healing are essential.

- ▸ **Reconciliation and Healing Programs:** Offering programs like confession services, retreats for healing, and support groups for individuals dealing with personal crises.

- ▸ **Mercy-Focused Messaging:** Emphasizing the themes of forgiveness, redemption, and unconditional love in outreach materials and communication.

Efforts should aim to reassure these individuals that no matter how great their struggle, the Church is a place of healing and restoration.

When communicating with struggling individuals, it's important to use language that conveys compassion, mercy, and the possibility of redemption. The goal is to help them feel welcomed back into the Church, no matter the extent of their struggle.

- ▸ **Offering Compassion:** "We understand that life's challenges can feel overwhelming. Please know that our Church is here to offer you compassion, support, and guidance on your journey to healing."

- ▸ **Encouraging Reconciliation:** "No matter what you've been through, God's love and mercy are always available to you. We invite you to seek peace through the sacrament of reconciliation."

- ▸ **Providing Support:** "You don't have to face this alone. We offer confidential counseling and spiritual direction to help you find your way back to the love and peace of Christ."

This language reassures struggling individuals that the Church is a place of refuge and healing, and that they are not alone in their struggles.

This spectrum again illustrates the diverse stages of faith and spiritual development that a parish office may need to consider when planning and implementing programs and initiatives. Keep in mind that having received the sacraments does not necessarily mean that a person is a disciple of the Lord. They might have a very superficial understanding and no personal relationship with God. The goal is to meet each individual where they are in their journey and provide appropriate support, resources, and opportunities for further growth and engagement in the faith community so that they develop their personal relationship with the Trinity.

By understanding this spectrum, pastors and parish leaders can more effectively tailor their approaches to evangelization, catechesis, and pastoral care. They can create a welcoming environment that invites individuals at various stages to explore, deepen, and live out their faith within the community.

Moreover, recognizing the fluidity of faith journeys is crucial. An individual's position on the spectrum is not fixed; rather, it is a dynamic process of growth, questioning, and transformation. People can go both forward and backward in their journey. The parish's role is to accompany and support individuals as they navigate the joys and challenges of their unique paths, always pointing them towards a deeper relationship with Christ and His Church.

Growing Believers

The "Growing Believer" group consists of individuals who have moved beyond the initial stages of discovering the Catholic faith and are now actively working to deepen their understanding and practice of it. These individuals have a basic foundation in Catholic teachings and are increasingly focused on integrating those beliefs into their daily lives. They seek to grow spiritually by participating more fully in the life of the Church and developing a stronger personal connection to God through sacraments, prayer, and community engagement.

Growing believers are on a spiritual journey where they are committed to learning and living out their faith more intentionally. They are eager to go deeper into Catholic doctrine and apply it to their personal and communal lives.

- ▸ **Definition:** Individuals actively deepening their understanding of the Catholic faith, working to live out Catholic teachings in their everyday lives.
- ▸ **Worldview:** These believers are committed to integrating faith into their daily routine and are seeking a more profound connection with the Church and its community.

Their worldview is increasingly centered around Catholic teachings, as they strive to align their personal values and actions with the tenets of the faith. They are open to deeper theological insights and seek to fully participate in the spiritual and communal life of the Church.

Growing believers are highly motivated by their desire to deepen their spiritual understanding and become more active participants in the life of the Church. They value community, personal growth, and a deeper relationship with God, and they seek to embody their faith in practical ways through service and sacramental participation.

- ▸ **Values:** A commitment to spiritual growth, community involvement, and living out Catholic values in everyday life.
- ▸ **Motivations:** Driven by a desire to understand Catholic doctrine more deeply, participate more fully in sacraments, and integrate faith into both personal life and community involvement.

Their spiritual development is characterized by a hunger for knowledge and a desire to live in accordance with Christian principles, making them eager to engage in parish activities and ongoing faith formation.

Growing believers tend to consume content that challenges them to think more deeply about theology, scripture, and the moral teachings of the Church. They appreciate reflective and thoughtful communication that encourages them to contemplate their faith in a more mature and nuanced way.

- ▸ **Media Consumption:** Likely to engage with advanced catechetical materials, spiritual literature, Church encyclicals, and content on Catholic social teaching.

▸▸ **Communication Styles:** Prefer thoughtful, reflective, and challenging communication that encourages deeper understanding and contemplation of faith.

They are drawn to content that offers new insights into Catholic beliefs and practices, as well as opportunities to explore how their faith can inform their decisions, relationships, and actions.

There are many opportunities to engage growing believers, particularly through ongoing faith formation programs and activities that allow them to actively participate in the life of the parish. They are eager for experiences that deepen their knowledge and give them a chance to live out their faith in practical ways.

▸▸ **Ongoing Faith Formation**: Bible studies, faith formation classes, retreats, and workshops that offer deeper insights into Catholic teachings and help believers grow spiritually.

▸▸ **Active Community Involvement:** Involvement in parish ministries such as liturgical roles, catechesis, or social justice initiatives, which allows them to apply their faith in action and service.

Providing opportunities for them to serve and grow within the Church allows growing believers to feel more connected to their parish and the broader Catholic community.

Despite their enthusiasm, growing believers may face challenges as they attempt to fully integrate their faith into their everyday lives. Balancing the demands of daily responsibilities with a commitment to deepening their faith can be difficult, and they may struggle to find resources that are tailored to their intermediate level of understanding.

▸▸ **Balancing Faith with Daily Life:** Finding ways to integrate an evolving faith with the demands of work, family, and other responsibilities can be challenging.

▸▸ **Finding Appropriate Resources:** Locating resources that match their growing but not yet expert level of understanding of Catholicism.

Helping them navigate these challenges by providing the right resources and support can empower them to continue growing in their faith.

To effectively engage growing believers, parishes should offer intermediate-level educational content that challenges them while providing practical applications of Catholic teachings. Facilitating community building and mentorship can also help them deepen their connection to the Church and develop supportive relationships with other parishioners.

- ▸▸ **Intermediate-Level Educational Content:** Provide resources such as discussion groups on Church doctrine, scripture study sessions, and opportunities for theological reflection.
- ▸▸ **Mentorship and Community Building:** Facilitate connections with mentors or peer groups that offer guidance, support, and fellowship.

Offering opportunities for both intellectual and communal growth will help growing believers continue their spiritual journey in a meaningful and supportive environment.

When communicating with growing believers, it's important to use language that encourages deeper exploration of faith while also inviting them to participate more fully in the life of the Church. This group is eager to contribute to the community, so offering opportunities for involvement and leadership is key.

- ▸▸ **Encouraging Deeper Exploration:** "As you continue to grow in your faith, we invite you to explore the richness of Catholic tradition through our various study groups and spiritual formation programs."
- ▸▸ **Fostering Active Participation:** "Your growing faith can find expression in many of our parish ministries. We encourage you to consider how your talents and interests might contribute to our community."
- ▸▸ **Building Supportive Networks:** "Joining one of our small groups can be a wonderful way to share your journey with others who are also deepening their faith. Let's learn and grow together."

This language emphasizes both the personal and communal aspects of growing in faith, helping them feel supported as they deepen their understanding and engagement in parish life.

Active Parishioners

The "Active Parishioner" group is made up of individuals who regularly attend church services, participate in parish activities, and have a solid foundation in Catholic faith and practice. These parishioners are committed to their spiritual growth and the wellbeing of their parish community. They see the Church as central to their lives and are continually seeking ways to deepen their relationship with God and enhance their role within the faith community. This group plays a vital role in the parish, providing stability, leadership, and a strong sense of community.

Active parishioners are deeply committed to their faith and view the Church as an essential part of their personal and family life. They have a well-established understanding of Catholic teachings and practice, and they strive to live out their faith in meaningful ways, both within and outside the parish.

- ▸▸ **Definition:** Individuals who regularly attend Mass, participate in sacraments, and are engaged in parish activities.
- ▸▸ **Worldview:** These parishioners view the Church as an integral part of their spiritual and communal life, seeking not only to maintain but to deepen their faith and contribute to parish life.

They are devoted to the sacraments and view parish involvement as an extension of their personal and spiritual commitment to living out the teachings of the Church in everyday life.

Active parishioners are motivated by a desire to deepen their faith, build community, and live out Catholic teachings in their daily lives. They value service, spiritual growth, and the sense of belonging that comes with being part of a faith community.

- ▸▸ **Values:** Strong commitment to faith, service, and community involvement. They value the opportunity to live out their Catholic beliefs through both spiritual and practical engagement with their parish.
- ▸▸ **Motivations:** Seeking deeper spiritual fulfillment, meaningful connections within the parish, and opportunities to serve and contribute to the life of the Church.

They are motivated to serve the parish not just through attendance but by becoming actively involved in parish ministries, leadership roles, and community events.

Active parishioners are engaged in content that enriches their faith and understanding of Catholic teachings. They seek opportunities for deeper spiritual reflection and theological enrichment, & they appreciate communications that focus on community building & spiritual growth.

- ▸▸ **Media Consumption:** Engages with books, Church publications, and religious programming that deepen their understanding of Catholic theology and encourage personal growth.

- ▸▸ **Communication Styles:** Prefer communications that are informative, spiritually enriching, and community-oriented. They appreciate messages that speak to their desire for deeper engagement and connection within the parish.

They often seek out materials that provide deeper theological insights and challenge them to grow in their spiritual journey.

There are many ways to engage with active parishioners, particularly by offering advanced faith formation opportunities and inviting them to take on leadership roles within the parish. This group is well-positioned to serve as mentors, leaders, and active contributors to parish life.

- ▸▸ **Advanced Faith Formation:** Interested in deeper theological studies, retreats, and adult faith formation programs that challenge and enhance their understanding of the faith.

- ▸▸ **Leadership Roles:** Likely to take on leadership or mentorship roles within the parish, such as serving on parish councils, leading ministries, or facilitating small groups.

By providing these opportunities, parishes can help active parishioners feel more connected to the faith community and support their desire for spiritual growth.

Despite their commitment, active parishioners may face challenges in balancing their involvement in the parish with personal, family, and professional responsibilities. They may also struggle with finding deeper spiritual engagement beyond regular parish activities, leading to stagnation or complacency.

- ▸▸ **Time Constraints:** Balancing church involvement with the demands of work, family, and other responsibilities can be difficult.

▶▶ **Seeking Deeper Engagement:** While active in the parish, some may feel a desire for more spiritually challenging or fulfilling activities beyond the standard parish offerings.

▶▶ **Mistaking Engagement for Growth:** It's important to continue challenging them to grow, as some may feel they have "arrived" once they are engaged in parish life, potentially leading to spiritual complacency.

Recognizing these potential barriers and providing opportunities for continued growth and balance can help active parishioners stay engaged and spiritually fulfilled.

Effective communication to active parishioners should focus on offering them opportunities for deeper spiritual growth, leadership, and engagement. Parishes can empower these individuals by recognizing their contributions and encouraging them to take on more significant roles within the community.

▶▶ **Targeted Spiritual Growth Opportunities:** Offer programs and resources tailored to their advanced understanding and commitment, such as spiritual direction, theological discussion groups, or more advanced faith formation classes.

▶▶ **Empowerment for Leadership:** Encourage active parishioners to consider leadership roles within the parish, such as ministry coordination, parish council participation, or catechesis, and provide training and support for these roles.

These strategies can help them continue to grow in their faith while also making meaningful contributions to the parish community.

When communicating with active parishioners, it's important to use language that recognizes their commitment to the Church while also encouraging them to explore further opportunities for growth and leadership. This group is often ready for deeper involvement but needs to feel appreciated and challenged.

▶▶ **Recognition of Commitment:** "We appreciate your dedication to our parish community and invite you to explore these further opportunities for growth and leadership within our church."

▸ **Encouragement for Deeper Involvement:** "Your experience and faith journey make you an ideal candidate for roles such as [specific ministry/role]. We believe your involvement would greatly benefit our parish."

▸ **Fostering Community Ties:** "Join us for [event/program], where you can connect with fellow parishioners who share your passion for deepening their faith journey."

This language affirms their existing contributions while motivating them to continue growing and becoming even more involved in parish life.

Committed Disciples

The "Committed Disciple" group consists of individuals who are deeply committed to their Catholic faith and actively seek to live out the Gospel in all aspects of their lives. These individuals often serve in leadership roles within parish ministries, evangelization efforts, and community outreach. Their lives are guided by their faith, and they are continuously striving to grow spiritually, serve others, and spread the teachings of Christ. For committed disciples, the Church is not only a place of worship but a mission field where they actively work to bring the Gospel to life.

Committed disciples are deeply rooted in their faith and view the teachings of the Church as central to their daily lives. Their worldview is shaped by the Gospel, and they seek to align all their decisions, relationships, and contributions to the Church and wider community with their faith.

▸ **Definition:** Individuals deeply committed to their Catholic faith, actively seeking to live out the Gospel in all life aspects and often involved in parish ministries or evangelization.

▸ **Worldview:** Their faith permeates every aspect of their life, guiding their decisions, interactions, and how they contribute to the Church and wider community.

For these individuals, their commitment to the Catholic Church is not just a private matter but a public mission. They feel called to share their faith through word and action, dedicating time and energy to the work of the Church.

The values of committed disciples center on faithfulness to God, service to others, and living a life that reflects Gospel principles. They are motivated by a deep desire to grow spiritually, to serve their community, and to spread the teachings of Christ both within and beyond the parish.

▸ **Values:** Deeply value faithfulness, service, community, and living a Gospel-centered life.

▸ **Motivations:** Driven by a desire to grow spiritually, serve others, and spread the teachings of Christ.

These individuals are motivated by the Great Commission (Matthew 28:19-20) and feel a personal responsibility to share the love of Christ with others. They find fulfillment in leadership roles, service projects, and evangelization efforts that allow them to live out their faith.

Committed disciples engage with content that challenges them to go deeper in their understanding of theology, scripture, and Church teachings. They prefer communications that are theologically rich, inspiring, and that encourage them to continue growing in their faith and mission.

▸ **Media Consumption:** Engages with in-depth theological materials, Church teachings, papal encyclicals, and advanced spiritual literature.

▸ **Communication Styles:** Prefers thoughtful, meaningful, and theologically rich communications that challenge and inspire deeper spiritual understanding.

Their media consumption often includes reading Church documents, listening to Catholic thought leaders, and engaging in discussions on theology, spirituality, and the social teachings of the Church.

Committed disciples are often looking for more advanced opportunities for spiritual growth, leadership, and evangelization. They are eager to take on significant roles within the parish and are well-suited for leadership in ministries, mission work, or catechesis.

▸ **Ministry Leadership:** Often take on significant roles in parish ministries, such as leading prayer groups, teaching catechism, or coordinating community service initiatives.

▸ **Evangelization Efforts:** Actively involved in evangelization activities, sharing their faith with others and participating in mission work, both locally and abroad.

Providing them with opportunities for leadership and deepening their faith journey can help them continue their mission of service and evangelization.

Despite their commitment, committed disciples may encounter challenges in finding opportunities that challenge them or balancing their various roles in the Church with their personal lives. Offering them the right resources and support can help them overcome these barriers.

▸ **Finding Challenging Opportunities:** Seeking opportunities that continue to challenge and grow their faith in meaningful ways.
▸ **Balancing Roles:** Managing their commitment to various ministries and their personal, family, and professional lives.

Parishes should help them find new avenues for growth and offer guidance on maintaining a healthy balance between their ministry work and other life responsibilities.

To effectively engage committed disciples, parishes should offer advanced spiritual development programs, as well as empower them for evangelization and leadership. Recognizing their dedication and potential to lead can inspire them to take on more significant roles within the Church.

▸ **Advanced Spiritual Development Programs:** Offering retreats, workshops, and courses that provide deep theological and spiritual education.
▸ **Empowerment in Evangelization:** Providing resources and training for effective evangelization and community outreach.

By offering these resources and recognizing their contributions, parishes can support their continued growth and engagement with the mission of the Church.

When communicating with committed disciples, it's important to acknowledge their dedication to living out their faith and offer opportunities for further growth and leadership. These individuals are often looking for ways to continue growing spiritually while helping others in the community do the same.

▸ **Acknowledging Their Commitment:** "Your deep commitment to living out your faith is an inspiration. We invite you to share your journey and insights through [specific ministry/role]."

▸ **Encouraging Further Growth:** "As someone deeply rooted in your faith, you might find our advanced theological study groups both challenging and enriching."

▸ **Fostering Leadership and Mentorship:** "Your experience and wisdom are invaluable assets to our community. Consider mentoring others or leading initiatives that align with your passion for the Gospel."

This language recognizes their spiritual maturity while also encouraging them to continue their personal growth and leadership within the Church.

Spiritual Mentor / Leader

The "Spiritual Mentor/Leader" group consists of individuals who are experienced and mature in their faith, often taking on roles of mentorship, leadership, or teaching within the Church. This group includes catechists, deacons, lay leaders, and other dedicated parishioners who feel called to guide and support others on their spiritual journey. Their deep understanding of Catholic teachings and their commitment to living out the faith make them invaluable to the parish community. They are driven by a desire to pass on the faith, educate others, and nurture spiritual growth within the Church

Spiritual mentors and leaders possess a profound understanding of Catholic teachings, doctrine, and tradition. Their worldview is marked by their commitment to living out the faith in daily life and their dedication to helping others do the same.

▸ **Definition:** Experienced and mature individuals in faith who often take on roles of mentoring, guiding, or leading others in their spiritual journey, including catechists, deacons, and lay leaders.

▸ **Worldview:** A deep understanding of Catholic teachings coupled with a strong commitment to nurturing the spiritual growth of others.

These individuals see their faith as not just a personal belief but as a vocation to serve others in their journey toward God. Their role is often characterized by a sense of responsibility for the spiritual development of those they mentor and lead.

Spiritual mentors are driven by a strong sense of duty to pass on their faith and wisdom to others. They value spiritual growth, wisdom, and the tradition of mentorship, believing that helping others deepen their faith is a core aspect of their vocation.

- ▸ **Values:** Deeply value wisdom, spiritual growth, mentorship, and the responsibility to pass on faith traditions and teachings.
- ▸ **Motivations:** Motivated by a call to serve others, educate them in the faith, and foster spiritual growth within the Church community.

They often find personal fulfillment in seeing the growth of those they mentor and are committed to ensuring that the faith continues to flourish within the next generation of believers.

Spiritual mentors and leaders engage with content that challenges them intellectually and spiritually. They seek out theological writings, Church documents, and resources that help them deepen their own understanding while equipping them to guide others. Their communication style is often nurturing, insightful, and rooted in a desire to make complex theological concepts accessible.

- ▸ **Media Consumption:** Engages with a wide range of theological, spiritual, and ecclesial literature and media, seeking materials that offer deep insights into faith and pastoral care.

- ▸ **Communication Styles:** Prefer deep, insightful, and nurturing communication. They are skilled in conveying complex theological concepts in an accessible manner.

They are avid learners themselves, constantly seeking to expand their knowledge to better serve those they lead.

Spiritual mentors and leaders are often actively involved in teaching, leading, and guiding within the parish. They are eager to participate in programs that help them continue growing in their own faith while supporting others in their spiritual journeys.

- ▸ **Teaching and Mentorship:** Actively involved in roles such as leading OCIA programs, teaching religious education, and facilitating spiritual retreats.

▸▸ **Community Leadership:** Often hold leadership positions within parish committees, councils, and other church organizations, helping shape the direction of parish life.

Their leadership roles often extend beyond formal teaching, as they serve as spiritual guides and confidants to parishioners seeking deeper engagement with their faith.

Despite their strong commitment, spiritual mentors and leaders often face challenges in balancing their personal responsibilities with their leadership roles in the Church. They may also struggle to find opportunities for their own continued growth, as they are often focused on helping others.

▸▸ **Balancing Multiple Roles:** Managing their roles as mentors and leaders with personal, family, and professional responsibilities can be a challenge.

▸▸ **Continued Personal Growth:** Seeking opportunities for their own spiritual and theological growth to remain effective in their mentorship roles.

▸▸ **Finding Time for Personal Prayer:** Sometimes they are so relied upon by others in the parish that they are constantly called upon to help with ministries, leaving them with little time for their own personal prayer or Mass participation.

Ensuring that they have the resources and support to balance their many responsibilities is essential for their continued effectiveness as spiritual leaders.

Parishes can effectively engage spiritual mentors by offering them advanced educational opportunities and support for their leadership roles. Providing spaces for personal spiritual retreats, leadership training, and ongoing formation can help them continue growing while serving others.

▸▸ **Ongoing Education and Formation:** Offer advanced theological training, spiritual formation programs, and opportunities for personal retreats to support their own growth.

▸▸ **Leadership Development:** Provide resources and workshops that enhance their skills in leadership, pastoral care, and evangelization, ensuring they remain equipped for their roles.

These opportunities not only support their personal development but also empower them to lead and mentor more effectively within the parish.

When communicating with spiritual mentors and leaders, it's important to recognize their vital role within the community while offering continued support and opportunities for growth. These individuals need to feel valued for their contributions and encouraged to continue deepening their own spiritual lives.

- ▸ **Recognition of Their Role**: "Your experience and wisdom are vital to our community's spiritual growth. We value your contributions and leadership in our parish."
- ▸ **Encouraging Continued Growth:** "As a spiritual mentor, your ongoing formation is essential. We encourage you to participate in [specific program] to further deepen your knowledge and skills."
- ▸ **Supporting Their Ministry:** "Your role in guiding others is a blessing to our community. Let us know how we can support you in your valuable work."

This language shows appreciation for their role while offering them opportunities for continued development and support.

Saintly Aspirant

The "Saintly Aspirant" group consists of individuals who are profoundly committed to pursuing a deep, contemplative relationship with God. They strive to live lives marked by holiness, often characterized by a strong prayer life, self-sacrifice, and a desire to fully embody Christian virtues. These individuals prioritize spiritual growth and are motivated by a longing for closeness with God, aiming to align every aspect of their lives with the teachings of Christ and the Church. Their journey is often marked by seeking out opportunities for deeper spiritual formation and service to others.

Saintly aspirants seek a deep, transformative relationship with God, aspiring to live in accordance with the highest ideals of Christian holiness. Their worldview is rooted in a desire for spiritual perfection, and they focus on aligning their actions, thoughts, and prayers with the teachings of the Church.

- ▸ **Definition:** Individuals who strive for a deep, contemplative relationship with God, characterized by intense prayer, self-sacrifice, and a desire for holiness.

▸▸ **Worldview:** A life focused on spiritual growth, aligning every aspect of their existence with Christ's teachings and the Church's mission.

These individuals place great importance on living out the Gospel in every aspect of their lives, seeking to embody virtues like humility, charity, and patience.

Saintly aspirants place a high value on spiritual discipline, contemplative prayer, and service to others. They are motivated by a deep longing for closeness with God, the desire to grow in virtue, and to be a witness to the transformative power of a life lived in holiness.

▸▸ **Values:** Prioritize spiritual discipline, contemplative prayer, service to others, and living the Gospel in daily life.

▸▸ **Motivations:** Driven by a desire for closeness with God, spiritual perfection, and serving as a living witness to Christ's love and holiness.

Their spiritual journey is defined by a deep commitment to the practices of prayer, fasting, and acts of charity, as well as a profound desire to live a life fully dedicated to Christ.

Saintly aspirants engage with content that fosters spiritual growth and deepens their contemplative life. They seek out writings of saints, advanced theological texts, and contemplative literature that challenge them to go deeper in their faith. They also appreciate deep, meaningful conversations that center around spiritual growth.

▸▸ **Media Consumption:** Engages with advanced spiritual and theological texts, writings of saints, and contemplative literature.

▸▸ **Communication Styles:** Prefers deep, meaningful, and spiritually enriching conversations, often centered around theological insights and personal spiritual experiences.

Their spiritual reading and study habits reflect their deep desire to grow closer to God and live out the teachings of the Church with increasing authenticity and fervor.

There are many opportunities to engage saintly aspirants, particularly through spiritual retreats, workshops, and ministries that require a high degree of spiritual

maturity. They are often drawn to roles in service ministries and are eager to participate in activities that deepen their spiritual lives and help others on their journeys.

- ▸ **Spiritual Retreats and Workshops:** Actively seek out retreats, workshops, and conferences that focus on deepening spiritual life and understanding.
- ▸ **Service and Ministry:** Often involved in ministries that require compassion, dedication, and spiritual maturity, such as hospital ministry, counseling, or serving the underprivileged.

Providing opportunities for contemplative prayer and service-based ministry helps saintly aspirants live out their desire to embody the Gospel in their daily lives.

Despite their strong commitment to holiness, saintly aspirants can face challenges in finding a community of like-minded individuals or balancing their spiritual aspirations with the practical demands of everyday life. Additionally, they may feel pressure to always appear holy, rather than being authentic about their struggles.

- ▸ **Finding Like-Minded Community:** Locating a community or group that shares a similar depth of spiritual commitment and practice can be challenging.
- ▸ **Balancing Aspirations with Everyday Life:** Integrating their intense spiritual practices and aspirations with the demands of daily responsibilities can be difficult.
- ▸ **Not Being Real:** Sometimes saintly aspirants feel they can't let down their guard and be authentic. It's important for them to remember that holiness includes acknowledging and growing through one's trials and tribulations, not just putting on a façade of perfection.

Encouraging authenticity and helping them find a balance between their spiritual aspirations and their everyday lives can greatly enhance their spiritual journey.

Parishes can effectively engage saintly aspirants by offering programs that are focused on deep spiritual growth, such as directed retreats, contemplative prayer groups, and courses on mysticism. Providing opportunities for mentorship and creating supportive networks of like-minded individuals can also be instrumental in their spiritual development.

▸▸ **Targeted Spiritual Formation:** Offering programs and resources tailored to deep spiritual growth, such as directed retreats, spiritual direction, and courses on mysticism and contemplative prayer.

▸▸ **Creating Supportive Networks:** Facilitating connections with mentors, spiritual directors, and communities that support and nurture their aspirational journey.

These strategies help foster a deeper connection to the Church while providing saintly aspirants with the resources they need to continue growing in their spiritual lives.

Effective Language for Engagement

When communicating with saintly aspirants, it's important to use language that acknowledges their deep commitment to spiritual growth and encourages them to continue striving for holiness. They appreciate being supported in their journey and being given opportunities to deepen their relationship with God.

▸▸ **Encouraging Deeper Commitment:** "We recognize your deep commitment to spiritual growth and invite you to explore our contemplative prayer group to further deepen your journey."

▸▸ **Fostering Holistic Growth:** "As you seek to live a life of holiness, consider joining our service ministry, where your spiritual gifts can profoundly impact others."

▸▸ **Supporting Their Aspirations**: "Your aspiration for a saintly life is inspiring. Let us support you with resources and guidance to help you on this sacred path."

This language offers them the support and recognition they need while challenging them to continue growing in their faith and service to others.

Practical Strategies for Empathetic Parish Leadership

Empathy, or the ability to understand and share the feelings of another, is not always intuitive or easy to put into practice. It requires intentional effort, self-awareness, and a willingness to step outside one's comfort zone. Here are some practical

strategies that clergy, administrators, and volunteers can employ to cultivate empathy and effectively meet people where they are on their faith journey.

Know your sheep:

Most parishes have people who live within its physical boundaries as well as those who come from outside the boundaries. There are various assessments, such as the Catholic Leadership Institute's Disciple Maker Index, which help to know your current parishioners better. It is also important to know the physical boundaries of your parish and understand how many people live there. You can do an online zip code demographic search to find out more about those people your parish is called to evangelize: how many are there, what are their ages, race, income, housing, and even religious affiliations. Even though you might not have the bandwidth to serve them all now, these are your sheep, and you should be moving towards evangelizing them actively.

Active Listening:

One of the most fundamental skills in empathetic communication is active listening. This involves giving the speaker your undivided attention, listening not just to the words being said but also to the emotions and nonverbal cues. It means suspending judgment, asking clarifying questions, and reflecting what you've heard to ensure understanding. By practicing active listening, parish leaders can create a safe space for individuals to share their stories, struggles, and aspirations.

Perspective-Taking:

Empathy requires the ability to step into another's shoes and see the world through their eyes. This can be particularly challenging when dealing with individuals whose experiences, beliefs, or actions differ significantly from our own. However, by making a conscious effort to understand their perspective, we open the door to genuine connection and compassion. This might involve asking questions, reading about different experiences, or engaging in dialogue with those from diverse backgrounds.

Welcoming Language and Actions:

The language we use and the actions we take can either foster charity and a sense of belonging or create barriers and drive people away. Empathetic parish leaders are mindful of using language that is welcoming, respectful, and sensitive to the diverse experiences of their community. This extends to actions as well, such as ensuring that parish events and programs are accessible and relevant to individuals at various stages of their faith journey. Be sure to be aware of cultural differences as well as language barriers.

Collaborative Problem-Solving:

When faced with challenges or conflicts within the parish, an empathetic approach involves collaborative problem-solving. Rather than imposing solutions or making unilateral decisions, empathetic leaders engage the community in dialogue, seeking to understand different perspectives and working together to find mutually beneficial solutions. This not only leads to better outcomes but also fosters a sense of ownership and investment among parishioners. For priests from different cultures this can be particularly challenging, yet it is essential in today's world, no matter the country or culture we operate in.

Ongoing Formation and Self-Reflection:

Empathy is not a one-time achievement but a lifelong practice. To grow in empathy, parish leaders must commit to ongoing formation and self-reflection. This might involve participating in workshops or retreats focused on empathetic leadership, seeking mentorship from experienced leaders, or engaging in regular self-examination. By continuously learning and reflecting on one's own attitudes and behaviors, leaders can deepen their capacity for empathy and more effectively serve their communities.

Modeling Christlike Love:

Ultimately, empathy in parish leadership is rooted in the example of Christ himself. Jesus consistently met people where they were, offering compassion, understanding, and invitation. He dined with sinners, touched the untouchable, and offered hope to the marginalized. By striving to model Christ's love in all their interactions, parish leaders can create a culture of empathy that permeates every aspect of parish life.

By consistently practicing empathy, parish leaders can transform their communities into places of authentic welcome, growth, and discipleship. They can create an environment where individuals, regardless of their starting point, feel seen, heard,

and supported on their journey towards a deeper relationship with Christ and his Church.

As we navigate the joys and challenges of parish life, may we always remember the words of St. Teresa of Calcutta: "Not all of us can do great things. But we can do small things with great love." By approaching each encounter with empathy and love, we can make a profound difference in the lives of those we serve, one person at a time.

06

❝

"Miss no single opportunity of making some small sacrifice, here by a smiling look, there by a kindly word; always doing the smallest right and doing it all for love."

– – – –

ST. THÉRÈSE OF LISIEUX

Key Processes:

Processes Serve the Mission

> *"The secret of success is to do the common things uncommonly well."*
>
> **J.D. ROCKEFELLER**

At the heart of every thriving parish lies a set of well-oiled processes that support its spiritual mission. These processes, when designed and implemented thoughtfully, can transform the way a parish operates, ensuring efficiency without sacrificing the personal touch that makes a faith community unique.

For Catholics, the sacraments are the primary means of grace, the main way we receive God's love. Yet, balancing the administrative aspects of sacramental preparation with pastoral care can be challenging. One excited new father learned this lesson the hard way when he and his wife asked their parish about getting their child baptized. Excited about this significant milestone in their family's faith journey, he eagerly filled out the online application form provided by our parish. The automatic email response he received, however, left him feeling anything but enthusiastic.

Reading through the response, it was a cold, bureaucratic list of requirements. There wasn't a single word acknowledging the joyous occasion. It felt like a punch to the gut, turning what should have been a moment of celebration into an administrative hurdle. He knew the staff member in charge of baptisms and could tell there was a disconnect between their love for Jesus and the sacraments and the automatic response he had received upon submitting the online form.

This experience highlights a critical aspect of parish management: the need for processes that are efficient and pastoral. It's a delicate balance but one that's essential for nurturing a vibrant faith community.

Trust the Process, Not the Person

In parish administration, well-documented processes are invaluable. They ensure consistency, aid in training new staff, and prevent the loss of institutional knowledge when key personnel leave. Effective processes help you make decisions faster and better, without having to say "no" as often. This saves time and energy, allowing parish staff to focus on more critical aspects of their ministry.

When done right, good processes deliver better results more consistently. They eliminate the need to rely solely on individuals with historical knowledge, making the parish more resilient to staff changes. This is particularly important in a church setting, where clergy and lay staff may rotate more frequently than in other organizations. Additionally, when things break down, which will happen eventually, we can look to be critical of the process in a blameless retrospective and talk about how the process failed. At times, the process will need to be fixed, or another issue may need to be addressed. This may include addressing the action of a person, all while maintaining their dignity and humanity.

Consider the annual preparation for Holy Week. A comprehensive process document could transform this potentially overwhelming task into a manageable series of steps. It would outline everything from ordering palms to scheduling extra confessions, ensuring no detail is overlooked, regardless of who's in charge.

However, processes aren't just about efficiency. They're also about continuity and consistency. They ensure that whether you're a long-time parishioner or a newcomer, your needs are met with the same level of care and attention. They provide a framework for training new staff members, clergy included, smoothing transitions, and maintaining consistency in parish operations.

Recently, a parishioner shared why they changed parishes. The parish office said they couldn't issue a refund for an incorrect school payment promptly. This was a lot of money for the family, and by the time the refund came through, they felt abandoned and unimportant. Luckily, they remained Catholic and continued attending Mass, just in a different parish. Although the parish wasn't technically wrong, this story underscores how even seemingly minor administrative processes can have profound pastoral implications.

Implementing robust processes doesn't mean losing the human touch. Rather, it frees up time and mental energy for more personalized interactions. When routine tasks are streamlined, staff can focus on building relationships, offering spiritual guidance, and addressing unique needs within the community.

In the context of sacramental preparation, a well-designed process could have transformed my baptism application experience. Imagine if, instead of a cold list of requirements, I had received an automated response that included warm congratulations along with the necessary information. This could have been

followed up by a personal call from a parish staff member, combining efficiency with genuine pastoral care.

Documenting Processes

While it might be tempting to document every minute detail of parish life, such an approach would quickly become unwieldy. Instead, focus on the vital few rather than the trivial many. Start with processes that are essential to your parish's mission and daily operations. Here is the list of the most important ones but not necessarily in order of importance.

1. Sacramental Administration

The primary mission of the Church is the spiritual care of souls, and the administration of the sacraments is at the heart of this mission. This process includes scheduling and preparing for Masses, baptisms, confirmations, marriages, and funerals. Each sacrament involves specific liturgical and pastoral care requirements, including record-keeping (baptismal and marriage registers), preparing parishioners (RCIA, marriage preparation), and ensuring that all canonical guidelines are met. The sacraments are the lifeblood of parish life, and ensuring they are administered reverently and in accordance with Church teaching is essential.

2. Financial Stewardship and Budgeting

Good financial stewardship is essential to support the pastoral mission and operational needs. This includes budgeting, tracking donations and other revenue sources, managing expenses, and overseeing parish assets. The finance council plays a key role here, ensuring that the parish's financial resources are used wisely and transparently. Regular financial reporting, annual audits, and adherence to diocesan guidelines are critical to maintaining trust with parishioners and ensuring long-term financial sustainability.

3. Parishioner Engagement and Evangelization

Engaging parishioners and fostering a sense of community is central for the vitality of any parish. This process involves organizing outreach efforts, ministries, and faith formation programs (such as youth ministry, adult catechesis, and OCIA). It also includes fostering personal connections with parishioners through pastoral care, regular communications, and special events. Building a strong parish community is not just about getting people through the doors but helping them grow in their faith and become missionary disciples. Effective evangelization also involves outreach beyond the church walls, engaging with the wider community to fulfill the parish's mission.

4. Volunteer and Staff Management

A well-run parish relies on a mix of paid staff and volunteers to fulfill its mission. The process of recruiting, training, and managing staff and volunteers is essential to ensure that ministries run smoothly and effectively. This includes setting clear expectations, providing regular feedback, offering ongoing training, and ensuring that everyone is aligned with the parish's mission. Volunteers, in particular, require special attention, as their contribution is motivated by faith and service rather than financial compensation, making recognition and support even more critical.

5. Facility and Maintenance Management

The physical upkeep of the parish, including the church, parish hall, offices, and surrounding property, is an important operational process. This process includes regular maintenance, cleaning, and repair of the buildings, ensuring that they are welcoming, safe, and functional for liturgical and community events. It also involves managing major projects such as renovations or expansions. A well-maintained parish facility supports the spiritual and community life, creating an environment where parishioners feel welcomed and engaged.

6. Faith Formation and Religious Education

Religious education and faith formation are vital to the spiritual development of children and adults. This includes running programs like religious education, sacramental preparation, adult catechesis, OCIA, and Bible studies. Faith formation helps to deepen the understanding of the Catholic faith, fostering lifelong discipleship. A well-organized and engaging religious education process ensures that parishioners of all ages grow in their knowledge and love of God and the Church.

7. Pastoral Care and Counseling

Providing pastoral care to parishioners is an essential function. This includes offering spiritual guidance, visiting the sick and homebound, providing marriage and grief

counseling, and addressing the spiritual and emotional needs of parishioners. Pastoral care often happens informally but should be part of an intentional process to ensure that no one in the parish is spiritually neglected. This process supports parishioners through life's challenges and helps them stay connected to their faith and the parish community.

8. Liturgy Planning and Coordination

While sacramental administration is a core process, liturgy planning and coordination refers specifically to the preparation and execution of liturgical celebrations. This includes scheduling and preparing lectors, Extraordinary Ministers of Holy Communion, altar servers, sacristans, and the music ministry. Proper planning ensures that the liturgy is celebrated with reverence, beauty, and in accordance with Church norms. Liturgy planning also includes special services during Lent, Advent, and feast days, as well as ensuring that the liturgical calendar is faithfully followed.

9. Stewardship and Development (Fundraising)

For many parishes, stewardship and development are necessary to ensuring financial sustainability. This includes organizing annual appeals, capital campaigns, special collections, and promoting planned giving or endowment programs. The process of educating parishioners about stewardship as a form of discipleship—giving of their time, talent, and treasure—is essential for maintaining and growing the parish's resources. Successful stewardship goes beyond financial needs, fostering a culture of generosity that aligns with the Church's mission of service and outreach.

10. Compliance and Risk Management

Every parish must adhere to legal, financial, and diocesan compliance requirements to ensure safe and responsible operations. This process includes ensuring that all diocesan policies are followed (such as safe environment protocols for protecting children and vulnerable adults), managing insurance and liability coverage, and adhering to civil laws regarding employment, safety, and property management. Compliance and risk management are critical to protecting the parish from legal risks and maintaining a safe environment for parishioners and staff.

Other processes that are not essential for every parish, but that will be beneficial for growth, include:

➤ Branding and communications

➤ Social media and website management

➤ Community outreach programs

➤ Comprehensive discipleship pathways

➤ Data-driven ministry evaluation and planning

➤ Systematic staff and leadership development

➤ Recruitment processes

➤ Donor relations processes

These are the processes that can take your parish to the next level, moving from maintenance to mission. They require more sophisticated planning and execution but can yield tremendous fruits. Imagine a parishioner who stops donating because the online platform charged them double several months in a row and no one fixed the problem for them. That situation highlights the need for robust financial processes, even in areas we might consider "not essential".

Documenting the Processes

If you don't have any processes written out, begin by reaching out to other parishes. They might have a binder of SOPs, or Standard Operating Procedures, already. There's no need to reinvent the wheel when others may have already created effective process documents. Adapt their work to fit your unique circumstances. This collaborative approach not only saves time but also fosters a sense of community among parishes.

In the earlier story of the baptism application that got a cold email response, a well documented process, created from the "customer's" perspective, could have made all the difference. It could have ensured that every family received not just the necessary information but also the pastoral care and excitement their milestone deserved. This is the kind of process that falls squarely into the crucial 20% that gets you 80% of the fruit.

The goal isn't to create a bureaucratic nightmare but to provide clear guidance that empowers your team to serve more effectively. Well-documented processes should feel like a helpful roadmap, not a straitjacket. Exceptions can be made as necessary, and a documented process helps to have a more meaningful conversation about

when and how to make exceptions, using common criteria. For example, a family who is baptizing their third child in five years probably doesn't need to go through the same baptismal preparation that someone who hasn't been to church in ten years needs when they come to baptize their first child.

As you document these processes, always keep in mind the end-user - whether that's a parishioner, staff member, or volunteer. Does this process make their experience better? Does it reflect the love and care we want to show as a faith community?

When documenting these processes, consider their interconnections. For example, your sacramental preparation process might feed into your discipleship pathway. Your volunteer coordination could link with your leadership development efforts.

Where and How to Document the Process

Creating effective process documents isn't just about writing down steps. It's about crafting a tool that's user-friendly, comprehensive, and aligned with your parish's mission. The way you document and store these processes can make the difference between a dusty binder on a shelf and a living resource that truly guides your parish operations.

As for the "how," consider using a combination of text, flowcharts, and checklists. While linear checklists have their place, many parish processes are better represented as flow charts. This format allows for the complexity and nuance often required in pastoral work.

Use clear, concise language in your documentation. Avoid jargon and explain any technical terms because these documents may be used by new staff or volunteers who aren't familiar with church terminology. Even acronyms that seem obvious, such as OCIA, should be spelled out the first time they're used. Even better, include a glossary that spells out all the acronyms or uncommon words.

Include real-life examples or scenarios in your documentation. This can help users understand how to apply the process in different situations. For instance, in a process document for handling donation inquiries, you might include examples of how to respond to common questions or concerns.

Don't forget to date your documents and include a revision history. This helps ensure everyone is working from the most up-to-date version and allows you to track how processes evolve over time.

Lastly, make your process documents visually appealing. Use consistent formatting, include your parish logo, and consider using color-coding or icons to make the document more engaging and easier to navigate.

The goal is to create living documents that guide your parish operations, not rigid rules that stifle creativity and pastoral care. Well-documented processes should empower your team to serve more effectively and consistently, always with an eye towards your parish's mission and your community's needs.

Processes as a Flow Chart Rather than Linear

In our quest for simplicity, we sometimes *oversimplify*. This is particularly true in parish administration, where we're tempted to create one-size-fits-all processes. But life—and faith—rarely follow a straight line. This is where flow charts come into play, offering a more nuanced approach to parish processes.

Flow charts acknowledge the various paths people may take on their spiritual journey, allowing for flexibility without sacrificing structure. This approach is especially valuable in our post-Christian society, where individuals come to the Church from diverse backgrounds and with varying levels of faith formation

Take, for example, the process of marriage preparation. A linear process might look like this:

- ▶▶ Engagement,
- ▶▶ Initial meeting,
- ▶▶ Pre-Cana classes,
- ▶▶ Final meeting,
- ▶▶ Wedding

But what about couples who are already living together? Or those where one partner isn't Catholic? A flow chart can incorporate these scenarios, guiding pastoral staff to address specific needs while ensuring all necessary steps are covered.

In my own experience with the baptism application, a flow chart approach could have made a world of difference. Instead of a rigid checklist, imagine a process that first asked about the family's background and needs. Are they active parishioners? New to the faith? Returning after some time away? Based on these answers, the process could have branched out, offering personalized guidance and support at each step.

This flexibility doesn't mean compromising on essentials. Rather, it allows us to meet people where they are, echoing Christ's own approach to ministry. It transforms our processes from rigid rules into pastoral tools, helping us guide individuals and families along their unique faith journeys.

Again referring back to the story of the family who asked for a refund after an erroneous payment, a flow chart approach for handling financial matters could have included steps for expedited refunds in cases of financial hardship or a communication flow to keep the family informed of the refund status. This could have prevented the feeling of abandonment that led to their departure.

When creating flow charts, start with the ideal scenario, then add branches for common variations. Use decision points to guide users through different paths based on specific circumstances. For instance, in a sacramental preparation flow chart, you might have decision points like "Is the family registered with the parish?" or "Has the individual completed previous sacraments?"

Remember to include feedback loops in your flow charts. These allow for reassessment and adjustment if initial approaches aren't effective. For example, if a couple struggles with a particular aspect of marriage preparation, the process should allow for additional support or alternative approaches rather than simply halting progress.

Digital tools can be particularly useful for implementing flow chart processes. Many customer relationship management (CRM) systems allow for automated workflows that can guide staff through complex processes, ensuring no steps are missed and providing prompts for personalized interactions at key points.

By adopting a flow chart approach, we acknowledge the complexity of human experience and the diversity of faith journeys. We create processes that are structured and flexible, efficient and pastoral. This approach helps us fulfill our mission more effectively, ensuring that no one falls through the cracks and that each person receives the care and attention they need on their faith journey.

Training Processes

Once your parish's key processes are documented, the next step is to ensure that your team—whether they are employees, contractors, virtual assistants (VAs), or volunteers—are properly trained to follow them. Effective training helps everyone understand how to execute their roles, ensures consistency, and fosters accountability. While the overall goal is the same for each group, the training approach should be tailored to their specific roles, level of involvement, and responsibilities.

Here's how to approach process training for each group:

1. Training Employees: In-Depth and Ongoing

Employees are the core operational team of the parish, and they often handle multiple processes on a day-to-day basis. Therefore, training employees should be detailed and hands-on, with a focus on both understanding the process and knowing how to apply it in various situations.

Key Training Methods for Employees:

Formal Onboarding: New employees should undergo a structured onboarding program that includes an introduction to key processes, their role within them, and expectations for performance. Provide documented process guides or manuals for them to refer to as needed.

Hands-on Demonstrations: Conduct in-person or video-based demonstrations of how each process is executed. This helps employees not just see the steps on paper but actually understand how to carry them out.

Role-Specific Training: Tailor the training to each employee's role. For instance, a parish office manager may need detailed training on the financial stewardship process, while a director of religious education will focus more on faith formation and volunteer coordination.

Ongoing Review: Schedule regular review sessions, especially for complex processes. These check-ins allow employees to ask questions, clarify misunderstandings, and ensure they are following the documented process correctly.

Mentorship/Coaching: Pair new employees with seasoned staff who can mentor them through the process execution. This promotes learning in a real-world context and builds confidence in applying the processes correctly

2. Training Contractors: Clear Deliverables and Expectations

Contractors are typically brought in to complete specific projects or tasks. Since they are not involved in the day-to-day operations of the parish, training should be focused on setting clear expectations and ensuring they understand how their work fits into the parish's overall processes.

Key Training Methods for Contractors:

Clear Documentation: Provide contractors with the process documentation that applies to their project. For example, if a contractor is hired for a construction project, ensure they understand the parish's process for facilities management, budgeting, and approvals.

Project-Specific Orientation: At the start of the project, walk contractors through the process step by step, highlighting key deliverables and deadlines. Ensure they understand how their work fits into the broader operations of the parish.

Defined Milestones: Since contractors operate independently, provide clear milestones that align with the parish's process. For example, a contractor managing a new website should be given deadlines for design drafts, content uploads, and testing, tied to the communications process.

Check-Ins: Schedule regular check-ins to review progress, clarify any misunderstandings, and ensure that the contractor is following the process as intended. These check-ins also provide opportunities to address issues before they escalate.

3. Training Virtual Assistants (VAs): Task-Focused and Remote-Friendly

Virtual assistants (VAs), particularly those working offshore, typically handle specific administrative or operational tasks remotely. Their training needs to focus on clear, step-by-step instructions for the tasks they will handle within the broader process.

Key Training Methods for Virtual Assistants:

Task-Specific Documentation: Since VAs often work on discrete tasks, provide them with simple, step-by-step guides or checklists that explain each task in detail. Ensure that the instructions are clear and assume no prior knowledge of the process.

Video Training: Record screen-sharing or video tutorials showing how to complete tasks. For example, if the VA is responsible for updating a parish database, show them exactly how to log in, navigate the system, and input information correctly.

Regular Feedback Loops: Since VAs work remotely, it's important to have structured communication through email or task management platforms like Trello or Asana. Set up regular check-ins to review completed tasks, provide feedback, and correct any deviations from the process.

Simplicity and Clarity: VAs may not be familiar with the nuances of parish culture or operations, so keep training as simple and task-oriented as possible. Focus on clarity and simplicity in both the training materials and communication

4. Training Volunteers Mission-Driven and Flexible

Volunteers are motivated by service and may not have the same level of time commitment as employees. When training volunteers, it's important to keep the process of training simple, clear, and tied to the parish mission while respecting their availability.

Key Training Methods for Volunteers

Mission-Centered Orientation: When training volunteers, begin by explaining how their role fits into the overall mission of the parish. This gives context and helps volunteers see the value of following the process.

Hands-On and Visual Training: Provide quick, hands-on training sessions or simple visual guides (diagrams, flowcharts) to help them understand the processes they'll be involved in. For example, if they're helping with event planning, give them a visual timeline of the planning process and their specific responsibilities.

Group Training Sessions: Many volunteers prefer learning in a group setting, where they can ask questions and learn from others. Host group training sessions that are interactive and concise, focusing on the key steps of the process.

Task-Specific Support: Volunteers often need task-specific guidance, especially when they are new to the parish or the role. Assign a point person (such as a staff member or experienced volunteer) who can offer support, answer questions, and guide them as they learn the ropes.

Flexibility in Expectations: Volunteers may have limited availability, so provide flexible options for training, such as pre-recorded tutorials or written guides that they can review on their own time. Keep training sessions short and to the point, focusing on the essentials they need to know.

Tailoring Training to Each Group

Training processes is not a one-size-fits-all approach. Each group—employees, contractors, virtual assistants, and volunteers—requires tailored methods that reflect their level of engagement and responsibility within the parish. By providing clear, structured, and mission-aligned training, you ensure that each team member understands their role, follows the documented processes effectively, and contributes to the parish's overall mission.

The key is to deliver training that is accessible and practical for each group, with ongoing feedback and support to ensure that everyone is equipped to perform their role successfully.

Statistics support the importance of such attention to detail. According to a 2019 Pew Research Center study, 27% of U.S. Catholics who left the church cited dissatisfaction with their parish or church as a reason for leaving. This underscores the critical role that effective, people-centered processes play in nurturing a thriving faith community.

Managing and Reinforcing Processes

Once you've documented and trained your team on parish processes, the next step is ensuring these processes are managed and reinforced consistently. Proper management and reinforcement are crucial to maintaining the efficiency, effectiveness, and alignment of operations with its mission. Whether you're dealing with employees or volunteers, regular reinforcement helps maintain accountability, ensure adherence to standards, and improve overall performance

1. Ongoing Oversight and Monitoring

Effective management of processes begins with ongoing oversight. This means regularly checking that the processes are being followed as documented and that any deviations are identified and corrected promptly. The frequency and depth of oversight will vary depending on the complexity of the task and the person performing it (e.g., an employee versus a contractor or volunteer).

For Employees:

Regular Check-Ins: Schedule regular one-on-one meetings to discuss how processes are being followed and address any challenges. Employees need ongoing feedback to stay aligned and motivated.

Process Audits: Periodically review key processes with employees, especially in areas like financial stewardship, religious education, and pastoral care. This can take the form of process audits, where you evaluate whether steps are being followed and outcomes are being achieved. Your diocese might offer audits, which we suggest you accept or even request. Sometimes you may need an outside audit if your parish is larger or more complex.

Peer Reviews: Encourage employees to observe each other's work and offer feedback, ensuring that processes are consistently reinforced across the team. This also fosters collaboration and shared responsibility for quality.

For Contractors:

Milestone Reviews: Since contractors often work on specific projects, set clear milestones with regular progress reviews. Ensure that their work is progressing according to the process and make adjustments as needed.

Completion Checklists: Use detailed checklists to review project deliverables and verify that all required steps were followed.

For Volunteers:

Mentorship Programs: Pair new volunteers with experienced ones who can model how to follow parish processes. This not only reinforces the processes but also builds a sense of community and shared purpose.

Periodic Group Refreshers: Host group refresher sessions for volunteers where you revisit key processes, especially before major events or the start of a new ministry season.

2. Continuous Feedback and Process Adjustments

Reinforcement is not a one-time event. Processes must evolve, and teams should receive continuous feedback to ensure they're following them correctly and efficiently. It's equally important to listen to feedback from the team to improve the process.

Continuous Feedback Loops: Regularly provide constructive feedback and praise during team meetings, check-ins, and performance reviews. Reinforce the importance of following the processes by highlighting how their work contributes to the overall mission.

Process Adjustments: If employees identify inefficiencies or bottlenecks, be open to adjusting the process. This can be done through collaborative discussions or formal process improvement initiatives. Employees often have valuable insights into how processes work in practice, and their input can help refine and improve them.

Project Post-Mortems: After project completion, conduct a debrief or "post-mortem" to assess how well the processes were followed and what improvements can be made. This helps reinforce the value of structured processes and provides learning opportunities for future projects.

Recognition of Process Adherence: Publicly recognize volunteers who consistently follow processes well. Volunteers, unlike employees, are driven by their passion and desire to contribute, so showing appreciation for their adherence to procedures can reinforce positive behavior.

Gentle Course Correction: Volunteers may occasionally deviate from the process due to lack of training or understanding. Approach corrections with kindness and patience, framing feedback as a way to help them contribute even more effectively.

3. Accountability Structures

To ensure that processes are followed consistently, you need to establish clear accountability structures for each team member. Reinforcing processes through accountability doesn't just keep people on track; it also helps them understand the value of their work and its role in achieving the mission.

For Employees:

Ownership of Processes: Assign clear process owners for key areas such as financial reporting, sacramental preparation, or facility management. These individuals are responsible for ensuring the processes are followed and for addressing any issues that arise. This creates a sense of ownership and responsibility.

Performance Reviews: Incorporate process adherence into regular performance reviews. Evaluate employees not just on outcomes but also on how consistently and effectively they follow the documented processes.

For Contractors:

Contract-Based Accountability: Ensure contracts clearly outline process expectations. Hold contractors accountable for following established procedures, and tie their payments to project milestones that demonstrate process adherence.

For VAs:

Task-Based Metrics: Track VA performance using task completion metrics. Ensure they are following processes and meeting deadlines. Hold them accountable for delivering on-time, accurate results by regularly reviewing their task completion rate and adherence to process steps.

For Volunteers:

Team Leads: Designate team leaders among volunteers who can help hold others accountable for following processes. These team leads can act as "process champions" who ensure that tasks are completed according to the standards set by the parish.

4. Rewarding and Recognizing Process Adherence

Positive reinforcement is a powerful way to encourage consistent process adherence. Recognizing and rewarding team members who follow processes diligently helps build a culture of accountability and excellence.

For Employees:

Public Recognition: Acknowledge employees who consistently follow and improve processes during staff meetings or in parish communications. Recognition doesn't have to be elaborate—a simple "thank you" for a job well done can reinforce positive behavior.

Incentivize Improvement: Where appropriate, reward employees who not only follow processes but also suggest improvements. This can take the form of professional development opportunities, added responsibilities, or public recognition of their contributions.

For Contractors and VAs:

Positive Feedback and Referrals: Contractors and VAs often rely on good feedback and references for future work. Acknowledge their success in adhering to parish processes and offer to provide referrals or positive reviews as a way of rewarding good work.

For Volunteers:

Recognition and Celebration: Volunteers often appreciate public acknowledgment for their efforts. Hosting an annual volunteer appreciation event or featuring volunteers in parish bulletins or during Mass helps reinforce the value of their service and adherence to processes.

By establishing regular oversight, providing ongoing feedback, setting clear accountability structures, and reinforcing the importance of the processes in achieving the parish's mission, you create an environment where the technical and spiritual aspects of parish life flourish.

Improving Processes and Change Management

In parish life, every process—whether sacramental administration, financial management, or volunteer coordination—can be improved over time. A key part of successful parish management is recognizing that no process is ever perfect, and there is always room for improvement. However, discerning what to improve and when requires careful consideration, balancing urgency with importance and impact. A consistent approach to change management ensures that process improvements are thoughtful, strategic, and implemented in a way that enhances the parish's mission while minimizing disruption.

1. Assess the Need for Improvement Urgency vs. Importance

The first step in improving any process is to assess what needs improvement and determine whether the change is urgent, important, or both. Not every process requires immediate change, and it's critical to discern which areas will have the greatest positive impact on the parish.

Key Questions:

▸ **Is this change urgent?** Does this process pose an immediate challenge to parish operations, such as an outdated financial system that's causing errors?

▸ **Is this change important?** Will improving this process significantly enhance the parish's ability to fulfill its mission? For example, streamlining volunteer coordination may not be urgent, but improving it could greatly increase parishioner engagement and ministry efficiency.

▸ **What is the impact?** Will this improvement impact many aspects of parish life, or is it limited to a single area? Prioritizing changes with wide-reaching effects can amplify their positive impact.

Balancing urgency with importance allows you to prioritize improvements that will have the most meaningful and timely effect on the parish. For example, updating sacramental records might not feel urgent in the short term, but if it's preventing effective pastoral care or causing confusion, it becomes a high-priority improvement

2. Define the Scope and Impact of the Change

Once you've identified the process that needs improvement, it's important to define the scope of the change and understand its impact. Not every process needs a complete overhaul; sometimes, small tweaks can lead to significant improvements.

Steps for Defining Scope:

▸ **Identify** the specific steps that need to be changed. Is the problem with the entire process or just certain aspects of it? For example, if the parish's communication with parishioners is ineffective, is the issue the frequency of communication, the content, or the platform being used?

▸ **Assess** the ripple effects of the change. Will changing this process impact other processes or operations within the parish? For instance, improving the financial reporting process may also require changes in how donations are tracked or how the finance council reviews budgets.

▸ **Set clear boundaries** around what is being changed. By defining exactly what you're focusing on, you prevent the improvement effort from growing too complex or disorganized.

Defining the scope helps you manage the change efficiently, and understanding its broader impact ensures you address interconnected processes. For instance, improving the process for recruiting volunteers might also impact the training and retention processes, so those areas should be included in the improvement plan

3. Communicate the Change and Gain Buy-In

After defining the scope, the next step is to communicate the change to all those affected—employees, volunteers, contractors, and sometimes parishioners—and gain their buy-in. Effective communication fosters a shared understanding of why the change is necessary and how it will improve parish life.

Key Steps for Communication:

➤ **Explain the "why" behind the change:** Be clear about why this process is being improved. Is it to save time, reduce costs, improve parishioner engagement, or increase efficiency? For example, if you're improving the event planning process, explain how it will make it easier to organize events and foster greater parish participation.

➤ **Highlight the benefits:** Help your team see the advantages of the new process, not just in operational terms but also in how it aligns with the parish's mission. For example, improving the parish website might seem like a technical update, but the real benefit is how it will better engage parishioners and provide a welcoming experience for newcomers.

➤ **Set expectations:** Outline what will change, how it will affect their work, and the timeline for implementation. Transparency about expectations ensures that everyone is prepared and understands the impact on their role.

Effective communication creates buy-in by connecting the process improvement to the larger mission of the parish. For example, when introducing a new donation management system, make it clear that this change is not just about better accounting but also about enabling the parish to be more financially transparent and responsible, which in turn strengthens trust with parishioners.

4. Implement the Change Gradually and Provide Training

Once you've communicated the change, it's time to implement it in a gradual and manageable way. Large changes can feel overwhelming, so breaking down the implementation into smaller phases or steps can help ease the transition.

Steps for Implementation:

▸ **Pilot the change:** If possible, start with a pilot version of the new process. For example, if you're introducing a new volunteer scheduling tool, begin with one ministry before rolling it out to the entire parish. This allows you to identify any potential issues and refine the process before full implementation.

▸ **Provide training:** Ensure that those affected by the change receive proper training. Whether it's employees, volunteers, or virtual assistants, clear, hands-on training is essential for success. For instance, if you're improving how donations are tracked, provide training sessions for the finance team to ensure they understand how to use the new system.

▸ **Support during transition:** Be available for questions, feedback, and troubleshooting during the transition period. Change can be uncomfortable, but offering support reassures the team that they are not alone in adapting to the new process.

Gradual implementation allows for smoother transitions and reduces resistance. By training everyone involved and being available for support, you foster a sense of confidence and readiness for the change.

5. Evaluate, Adjust, and Reinforce the Change

Once the new process is in place, it's important to continuously evaluate its effectiveness and make any necessary adjustments. Improvement is an ongoing process, and regular evaluation ensures that the changes are truly benefiting the parish.

Key Evaluation Steps:

▸ **Monitor performance:** Track whether the process is delivering the intended improvements. Are tasks being completed more efficiently? Is communication clearer? For example, if you've streamlined the process for scheduling Mass volunteers, monitor how quickly and effectively schedules are being finalized.

▸ **Seek feedback**: Actively seek feedback from those using the new process. Are there areas where the change has created new challenges? Are there further tweaks that could make it more effective? Listening to feedback ensures that you catch any issues early and allows for continuous improvement.

▸ **Reinforce the change:** After evaluating the process, reinforce its importance by highlighting its success and ensuring that it remains a permanent part of the parish's operations. Celebrate small wins and acknowledge team members who have embraced the change effectively.

For instance, if the process improvement involved updating parish communications, track metrics like email open rates, parishioner engagement, or website traffic to evaluate whether the changes are having the desired effect. Reinforce successful outcomes by showing the team how their work has positively impacted the parish.

6. Balance Future Improvements

As new challenges and opportunities arise, continue to evaluate which processes should be improved next. Remember, not every process needs to be fixed at once, and maintaining a balance between urgency and importance ensures that improvements are made thoughtfully and with strategic intent. While it's tempting to address every inefficiency, focus on improvements that will have the highest impact on the parish's overall mission.

A Balanced Approach to Process Improvement

Improving processes in a parish is not just about solving operational problems— it's about continually aligning the parish's efforts with its mission and enhancing the experience for parishioners, staff, and volunteers. By balancing urgency with importance, communicating changes effectively, and managing implementation with care, you can ensure that process improvements have a lasting, positive impact.

Change management is not a one-time task but an ongoing part of parish leadership. With a consistent and thoughtful approach, you can ensure that processes evolve in a way that supports the spiritual and operational needs of the parish, helping it to thrive in its mission of serving the community.

Processes as a Reflection of Parish Culture

The processes discussed are more than just administrative tools. They are a reflection of your parish culture, a tangible expression of your values and priorities.

Effective processes should strike a balance between efficiency and pastoral care. They should be clear enough to ensure consistency and fairness yet flexible enough to accommodate the unique circumstances of each individual or family. We're not running a factory; we're nurturing a community of faith. Every interaction, every form, every email is an opportunity to reflect Christ's love to those we serve.

As we strive to create more effective processes, let's not lose sight of the bigger picture. Our ultimate goal isn't just to run a smooth operation but to build the Kingdom of God. Well-designed processes can free up time and energy for what really matters: nurturing faith, building community, and sharing the love of Christ.

In the words of management guru Peter Drucker, "The most important thing in communication is hearing what isn't said." As you develop and implement your parish processes, listen not just to what your parishioners are saying but to what they might be feeling or needing. Let your processes be a reflection of a parish that truly cares, that meets people where they are, and that always strives to embody the love of Christ.

07

CHAPTER

One-Year Priorities and Project Management

Management As
Mission

Purposeful Parish Leadership

Effective leadership in a parish requires more than just responding to immediate needs. To truly serve the spiritual and operational well-being of your community, you need a structured, thoughtful approach to planning and managing priorities. Annual planning allows you to step back, look at the bigger picture, and set a clear course for the year ahead. It aligns your parish's efforts with its mission and strategy, ensuring that every initiative, project, and process contributes to your overall goals.

This chapter will guide you through the essential components of annual planning, project management, and prioritization. You'll learn how to set and balance priorities for the parish as a whole, as well as for individual departments or ministries. We'll explore how to decide which initiatives will have the greatest impact and how to allocate resources efficiently to support them.

Additionally, we will cover practical tools for managing parish projects effectively— whether you're launching a new ministry, leading a capital campaign, or streamlining administrative processes. Finally, we'll discuss the balance between managing ongoing processes and completing time-bound projects, helping you maintain a rhythm that keeps the parish moving forward while staying grounded in its mission.

By the end of this chapter, you will have a framework for intentional planning, precise project management, and prioritizing what truly matters to ensure that your parish thrives—both spiritually and operationally.

It might seem overwhelming to add annual planning and project management to your already busy schedule, but you don't need an MBA or expensive software to get your parish aligned with the top priorities. In the following sections, we'll explore practical, accessible ways to set priorities, manage projects, and keep your parish moving forward. We'll look at how to conduct effective annual planning sessions, use simple tools for project tracking, and establish regular check-ins to ensure progress. The goal isn't to turn your parish into a corporation or lose sight of its spiritual mission. Instead, it's about using proven tools and techniques to help you fulfill that mission more effectively. By becoming more intentional about how you use your time and resources, you'll be better equipped to serve your parishioners, spread the Gospel, and build the Kingdom of God in your community.

Annual Planning

Here is a story about the power of annual planning from one of our clients (with his name redacted for confidentiality). Fr. Sam knew he was presiding over a collection of good intentions, not a parish on a mission. For three years, he felt the frustrating gap between his vision—a dynamic hub of missionary action—and the reality of scattered, disconnected efforts.

His solution was to stop the churn. He pulled his key leaders into a two-day retreat. Through prayer and honest conversation, they didn't just create a plan; they forged a new identity. One of their first, radical priorities was to halt all classroom-based religious education for an entire year. Instead, they would dedicate that time to prayer, intentionally walking with their catechists and mentoring them on their own faith journeys. It was a bold move, designed to discern how to rebuild their formation process around the whole family, not just the children.

The backlash to such a bold vision was immediate. Some staff, comfortable with the old ways, walked away. The Finance Council head, who believed a parish's business was anything but mission, quit in protest. It was a painful pruning, but a necessary one.

Fr. Sam and his core team held fast to the clarity they had fought for. They learned a crucial lesson: true unity isn't forced. By allowing people the freedom to say "no," the "yes" from those who remained became an unbreakable commitment.

That commitment became contagious. Ministry by ministry, the parish began to align. Today, Fr. Sam leads a focused, energized community, a testament to the fact that a clear plan, executed with courage, can change everything. His story is a powerful example of what strategic planning can unleash. But what does this process look like, and how can you implement it in your own parish?

The Structure of Annual Planning

Annual planning, coupled with quarterly check-ins, provides an excellent rhythm for strategic thinking and focused action. While this planning session can last anywhere from one to three days, depending on the size and complexity of your parish, the time you invest is crucial. As Abraham Lincoln said, "Give me six hours to chop down

a tree, and I will spend the first four sharpening the axe." This time spent planning is your axe-sharpening and it will make everything you do throughout the year more effective.

The basic structure for annual planning follows a three-part format:

- ▸▸ **What has happened?** (Review the past year.)
- ▸▸ **Where are we now?** (Assess the current state of the parish.)
- ▸▸ **What should we do next year?** (Set priorities for the coming year.)

However, this process is more than simply reflecting on the past and setting new goals. To ensure that your planning is effective, you must tie it back to the core processes discussed in chapter 6. These core processes are the operational backbone of your parish, and they must remain intact and functioning smoothly, even as you take on new projects.

In addition to core processes, the three to five major projects your parish will tackle in the coming year should be the result of careful discernment. This will be discussed further in this chapter, but it's important to recognize that your parish can only take on what it has the resources for in terms of time, talent, and treasure. As we discussed in the chapter on strategy, effective leadership often requires the discipline to say "no" to initiatives that don't align with your priorities or that overstretch your resources. Another way to say it is this: strategy is denial.

The Right Team and the Right Focus

Gathering the right people for your annual planning session is critical. Depending on your parish's size, this could be a mix of volunteers and paid staff or primarily paid staff for larger parishes. Aim to keep the group small—ideally no more than ten to twelve people, including your key leaders who have a broad view of the parish's operations.

It's often helpful to bring in an outside facilitator to lead the session, especially if you've struggled with effective planning in the past. As the pastor, this allows you to fully engage in the discussions without the added responsibility of guiding the meeting. A skilled facilitator can help keep the conversation focused, ensure that all voices are heard, and guide the team toward concrete decisions. More importantly, this enables you to step back and empower your team to contribute meaningfully, gaining their buy-in for the plan.

The primary outcome you're seeking from your annual planning session is a clear set of three to five parish-wide priorities or projects. These are the most critical initiatives that will help you move closer to fulfilling your mission and vision. But just as importantly, these priorities need to take into account the core processes that keep your parish functioning smoothly. Think of these core processes as the foundation, and the three to five major projects as the growth areas you will focus on for the year.

How to Decide on Priorities

Setting the right priorities is the heart of a successful year. It requires moving from broad vision to focused action. Here's how to build a plan that creates real impact:

- ▶▶ Begin with Prayer and Discernment. This is a spiritual process, not just a business meeting. Start by seeking God's guidance. Assess the genuine needs of your parishioners and the surrounding community to understand where He is calling you to invest your energy.

- ▶▶ Assess Your Landscape. To know where you're going, you must know where you stand.

  - ▶▶ **Look Backward:** What worked well last year, and what didn't?

  - ▶▶ **Look Inward:** What are your parish's unique strengths and talents?

  - ▶▶ **Look Outward:** What challenges and opportunities exist right now? This honest assessment will reveal the most fertile ground for your efforts.

- ▶▶ Choose Your Battles by Saying "No". True strategy is about making deliberate choices. You cannot do everything, so you must say "yes" only to the most critical initiatives. Limit your parish to three to five core priorities for the entire year. In fact, many of the most successful parishes find that focusing on just two or three truly essential goals yields the greatest impact. A shorter list beats a diluted one every time.

▸▸ Translate Priorities into High-Impact Projects. Every priority should be attached to specific, actionable projects. Aim for a total of three to five key projects for the year, with each priority having at least one dedicated project. A project can be:

> ▸▸ Improving a core process (like parish communications).
>
> ▸▸ Launching a new ministry or outreach initiative.
>
> ▸▸ Beginning a major undertaking (like a capital campaign or facility planning).

▸▸ For each project, define what success will look like. Answering "How will this transform our parish?" ensures you're focused on lasting impact.

▸▸ Fuel the Mission with Realistic Resources. A plan is only viable if it is resourced. For every project you commit to, you must be able to assign the necessary time, talent, and treasure. This is the moment of truth: if an initiative is truly a priority, it must be reflected in your parish's budget and calendar. If it doesn't have dedicated funding and protected time on the schedule, it's not a priority—it's just make-believe.

A Shared Vision for the Whole Parish

Annual planning isn't just about setting parish-wide goals—it's also an opportunityfor individuals and departments to align their own priorities with the parish's overarching direction. Encourage each department, ministry, and team member to develop their own annual goals that support the overall mission and key initiatives of the parish. This alignment ensures that everyone is working toward the same end, creating a unified and focused parish community. Finally, remember that annual planning is about setting a clear direction for the year, but it's not meant to be a rigid or unchangeable plan. Flexibility is important as you navigate the year ahead. The purpose of this process is to help you and your team focus on what matters most, providing a shared vision that will guide your decisions, actions, and resource allocation throughout the year. Importantly, this process also helps your team confidently say "no" to initiatives that don't align with your mission or current priorities.

By engaging in annual planning and prioritizing the core processes and key projects that will have the greatest impact, you set the foundation for a thriving parish that is equipped to fulfill its mission, serve its people, and grow in its spiritual and operational vitality.

There is an example of a two-page annual plan in the accompanying workbook.

Project Management: Turning Priorities into Action

Now that we've established our priorities through annual planning, it's time to focus on implementation, which is where effective project management comes into play. Many parishes struggle to implement ideas effectively. You may have experienced this: a flurry of excitement and ideas at a parish council meeting, only to see those plans fizzle out in the weeks that follow. This is where the real work begins. Implementation is 90% of the battle, and it requires deliberate effort and skill.

Think of ideas like seeds: they have great potential but need the right conditions to grow. Implementation is the process of preparing the soil, planting the seed, watering it regularly, and tending to it as it grows. It's not always glamorous, but it's essential for turning ideas into a fruitful harvest for your parish.

One of the key tools for effective implementation is project management. Many parishes struggle with this—few have staff trained in project management techniques, and even fewer use dedicated tools or software to track and manage projects. This often leads to disorganization and missed opportunities. As Michael Gerber, author of The E-Myth Revisited, emphasizes, "Systems run the business, people run the systems." In a parish context, project management is the system that helps turn your parish priorities into tangible results, ensuring that you can achieve meaningful progress without getting overwhelmed by the complexity of each task.

Breaking Down Each Project: Planning for Success

Once you've selected your key projects, it's important to break each one down into manageable steps. For each project, ask the following questions:

▶▶ **Who is responsible?** Identify a clear owner for each project—preferably not the pastor. This person will be accountable for driving the project forward and ensuring tasks are completed on time.

▸ **What does success look like?** Define the measurable outcomes for each project. Be specific about what success means and how you will know when the project has been successfully completed.

▸ **What are the key steps?** List out the main steps needed to complete the project. While it's helpful to outline the entire year's plan, at a minimum, you should plan the first ninety days in detail.

▸ **What are the deadlines?** Assign deadlines to each step or task. Establish a clear timeline for the project and ensure that each team member understands their deadlines and responsibilities.

Let's consider a hypothetical example to illustrate this approach:

Project: Increase Youth Engagement in the Parish

▸ **Person Responsible:** Deacon Mark

▸ **Success Description:** By the end of May next year, increase youth (ages 13-18) participation in parish life by 50%, as measured by attendance at youth-focused events and Mass attendance.

Key Steps for the First 90 Days:

1. Form a youth ministry team (Due: September 1, Responsible: Deacon Mark)

2. Conduct a survey of parish youth to understand their interests and needs (Due: September 15, Responsible: Youth Ministry Team)

3. Develop a six-month calendar of youth-focused events (Due: October 1, Responsible: Youth Ministry Team)

4. Plan and execute a youth ministry kickoff event (Due: October 15, Responsible: Youth Ministry Team with Parish Council support)

5. Review initial feedback and adjust plans as needed (Due: November 1, Responsible: Deacon Mark with Pastor and Youth Ministry Team)

This level of detail ensures that the project can move forward systematically, with clear responsibilities and measurable outcomes. While it might seem daunting to create such detailed plans, it's critical to keep everyone aligned and moving in the same direction. Breaking down large projects into smaller, manageable tasks helps the team make steady progress.

Establishing a Rhythm for Project Management

Once your key projects are underway, it's essential to establish a consistent rhythm for managing them. Regular check-ins and accountability structures are key to ensuring that progress is steady and that any roadblocks are addressed before they derail the project.

Here's a suggested structure for keeping projects on track:

1. **Quarterly reviews:** Every ninety days, bring your leadership team back together for a half-day or full-day offsite meeting. This allows time for prayer, reflection, and strategic thinking while reviewing progress on your key projects. Adjust priorities as needed and create updated plans for the next quarter.

2. **Monthly or weekly leadership meetings:** Use these meetings to check in on the progress of your key projects. Make sure each project owner provides updates on their responsibilities, and identify any obstacles or additional resources needed to keep the project moving forward. Each week should answer the following questions:

    a. What will get done this week?

    b. Who will do it?

    c. What resources do others need to provide to make it happen?

3. **Ad-hoc project meetings:** For particularly complex or time-sensitive projects, you may need to hold specific meetings with the project team to work through issues or coordinate next steps.

Consistency is the key to project success. Regular reviews and check-ins keep the team focused, prevent procrastination, and ensure that your projects don't get lost in the day-to-day busyness of parish life.

Tracking Progress: Keep It Simple

To successfully manage multiple projects, you need a simple and effective system for tracking progress. The key is to have one centralized location—whether a physical project board, a digital tool like Trello, or a shared spreadsheet—where

tasks, deadlines, and responsibilities are clearly laid out and accessible to all team members.

A good tracking system includes:

- ▶▶ Clear project milestones
- ▶▶ Task owners and due dates
- ▶▶ A place to record progress updates
- ▶▶ A method for flagging issues or delays

This doesn't need to be a complex or expensive system—what's important is that everyone knows where to go to see what needs to be done and by whom. Keeping everything in one place avoids confusion and keeps everyone accountable.

Focus and Commitment: No Superseding Projects

It's important to remember that the three to five key projects you select for the year are the **most important** for the entire parish. While individual staff or volunteers may take on additional, smaller projects, **none should take precedence** over these top parish priorities. The leadership team needs to stay laser-focused on completing these key projects, ensuring that they have the time, attention, and resources they need to succeed.

Taking on too many projects, or allowing less important initiatives to supersede the top priorities, leads to fragmentation and burnout. The projects you select must align with your mission, and your team must remain committed to completing them before diverting energy elsewhere.

Conclusion: Steady Progress, Big Results

One of the keys to successful project management is making steady, incremental progress. It's easy to become overwhelmed by the scope of a large project, leading to procrastination or loss of focus.

As the saying goes, "How do you eat an elephant? One bite at a time." Each step forward, no matter how small, moves you closer to realizing your parish's mission and goals.

Tools and Techniques for Effective Project Management

As we dive deeper into the practical aspects of project management, it's important to remember that these tools and techniques are meant to serve your mission, not complicate it. Think of them as the trellis that supports a growing vine - they provide structure and direction, allowing your parish initiatives to flourish.

Let's start with a fundamental tool: **the project tracker**. This can be as simple as a whiteboard or a spreadsheet or as sophisticated as dedicated project management software. The key is to have one centralized place where all project information is stored and easily accessible to your team.

A basic project tracker should include the following columns:

1. Task description
2. Person responsible
3. Due date
4. Status (Not started, In progress, Completed, Stuck, Waiting, Pushed)
5. Notes or updates

For smaller parishes or those just starting with formal project management, a whiteboard or a spreadsheet can be an excellent tool. It's familiar, easy to use, and doesn't require any additional cost. You can use Google Sheets for easy sharing and real-time collaboration among team members.

As your parish grows or your projects become more complex, you might consider investing in project management software. Popular options include Asana, Monday. com, Trello, and many others. These tools offer features like task dependencies, Gantt charts, and automated reminders. While they often have a cost associated with them, many offer discounts for non-profit organizations.

The tool itself is less important than how you use it. As Gino Wickman, author of *Traction*, often emphasizes, "What gets measured gets done." Regularly updating and reviewing your project tracker is crucial for keeping initiatives on track.

Another essential technique is time blocking. This involves scheduling specific times in your calendar for project work. It's all too easy for urgent but less important tasks to crowd out the time needed for strategic priorities. By blocking off time in advance, you're more likely to make consistent progress on your key initiatives.

For example, you might block off every Tuesday afternoon for work on your youth engagement project. During this time, you focus solely on tasks related to this priority, free from other distractions. This dedicated time can be incredibly productive and helps ensure that your most important work doesn't get pushed aside by day-to-day demands.

Should we hire a project manager? For most parishes, a dedicated project manager isn't necessary or financially feasible. Instead, project management should be seen as a skill set that all leaders in your parish can develop. By spreading this responsibility, you create a culture of accountability and empowerment.

To illustrate this, let's revisit Fr. Sam's story. After his successful planning session, Fr. Sam didn't hire a project manager. Instead, he invested time in training his team on basic project management skills. He didn't do this himself but had them attend a one-hour talk from a professional, then watch follow-up videos on YouTube. He introduced a simple project tracker and the concept of the Level 10 Meeting. At first, it felt awkward and time-consuming. But after a few weeks, the team began to see the benefits. Projects moved forward more consistently, and there was less confusion about who was responsible for what. Team members felt more empowered to take initiative, knowing they had a clear framework for tracking and reporting progress.

It's worth noting that project management in a parish setting doesn't need to feel corporate or impersonal. In fact, it can and should be infused with your spiritual mission. For example, you might start each project meeting with a brief prayer or reflection. You could include a "mission impact" column in your project tracker, reminding everyone of how each task connects to your larger purpose.

You'll likely need to adjust and refine your approach over time. The key is to start somewhere and consistently work at improving your processes.

The Power of Delegation

Delegation is one of the most important skills for effective leadership, especially in a parish setting where time and resources are often limited. It's the practice of entrusting tasks and responsibilities to others so that the leadership team—particularly the pastor—can focus on higher-level priorities. Effective delegation allows you to manage both the core processes and major projects of the parish without becoming overwhelmed or distracted by the day-to-day operations.

Why Delegation is Important

▸▸ **Maximizes efficiency:** By empowering others to take ownership of specific tasks or projects, you free up time for the most critical leadership and pastoral duties. This ensures that you can focus on strategy and mission rather than getting caught in administrative tasks.

▸▸ **Develops your team:** Delegation is also an opportunity for growth. It allows your staff, volunteers, and ministry leaders to develop their own skills and take on greater responsibility. Over time, this builds a stronger, more capable team that can carry out the parish's mission independently.

▸▸ **Increases parish capacity:** By spreading tasks across a team, you ensure that more gets done and that no single person (including you) is overburdened. This enables the parish to tackle both ongoing processes and major projects without falling behind.

How to Delegate Effectively

▸▸ **Define the task:** Be clear about what needs to be done, why it's important, and what the desired outcome looks like. The person you're delegating to should understand the scope of the task and its importance within the broader parish mission.

▸▸ **Select the right person:** Choose a delegate based on their skills, experience, and capacity. Not every task should be delegated to the same person. Newer team members may be more suited to smaller or clearly defined tasks, while experienced leaders can handle more complex responsibilities.

▸ **Set clear expectations:** Outline specific goals, timelines, and responsibilities. Make sure the person understands the task and the outcomes you expect and agrees on deadlines and checkpoints to track progress.

▸ **Provide the right resources:** Ensure that the person has the tools, information, and support they need to complete the task successfully. This could involve providing training, access to certain materials, or guidance on where to seek additional help.

▸ **Monitor progress:** Check in regularly to offer feedback, provide support, and address any obstacles. With new delegates, this might mean more frequent check-ins, while with experienced and trusted leaders, a lighter touch may be sufficient.

▸ **Hold them accountable:** Ensure that the person you delegate to knows they are responsible for the task. This includes meeting deadlines, producing the expected results, and communicating any challenges along the way. Regular follow-ups are essential to keep the delegate accountable.

Delegating to a New Delegatee vs. Trusted Delegatee

When delegating to a **new delegatee**, such as a volunteer or a staff member who is taking on this responsibility for the first time, it's important to provide **more guidance and oversight.**

▸ **Explain tasks in detail:** Go over each step of the task and explain why it's important.

▸ **Set up regular check-ins:** More frequent check-ins help ensure they stay on track and feel supported in their new role.

▸ **Offer mentorship:** Pair them with a more experienced team member who can offer guidance and answer questions.

▸ **Encourage learning and growth:** Be patient and use this delegation as an opportunity to teach them new skills. Understand that new delegates may need time to grow into their roles.

On the other hand, when delegating to a trusted and experienced delegatee, such as a seasoned staff member or volunteer leader, you can give them more autonomy.

➤ **Provide high-level guidance:** Since they already have experience, you don't need to go into as much detail. Focus more on the outcomes and overall objectives rather than the specifics of how to achieve them.

➤ **Fewer check-ins:** With trusted leaders, you can check in less frequently, giving them the freedom to manage their work independently.

➤ **Empower them to make decisions:** Trusted delegates should have the authority to make decisions within the scope of their task. Trust their judgment and allow them to problem-solve without your direct involvement, while still being available if they need advice.

Seeing Delegation Through

Always **circle back** to the person you've delegated to, review the completed work, and provide feedback. Recognize successes and address any areas for improvement. This ensures that tasks are completed to the desired standard and that you and your team members learn from the experience.

By delegating well, you not only lighten your own load but also empower your team, build up their skills, and foster a stronger sense of ownership and commitment to the parish's mission.

Balancing Core Processes and Top Projects: The Art of Disciplined Leadership

Balancing the parish's **core processes** and the **top three to five projects** for the year requires a delicate blend of intentionality, discipline, and flexibility. It is a challenging yet essential task for any parish leader, as both the ongoing operational tasks and the high-impact projects are critical to fulfilling the parish's mission. The key is developing a mindset that allows you to manage time, money, and other resources effectively, while remaining focused on your priorities without losing sight of the need to remain open to the Holy Spirit's guidance.

The Mindset of Balanced Leadership

First and foremost, successful leaders in the parish must adopt a mindset of **balance and intentionality.** Managing the **core processes**—the daily, essential functions like sacramental preparation, financial stewardship, and volunteer coordination—

requires constant attention to ensure that the parish continues to run smoothly. However, without dedicating time and focus to the **three to five key projects** identified during annual planning, the parish will remain in maintenance mode, unable to grow or respond to new opportunities.

The mindset needed here is one that recognizes both the **urgency of the present** and the **importance of the future**. Core processes are like the lifeblood of the parish, keeping it alive day to day, while the projects represent the growth and evolution that will bring your parish closer to its long-term vision. Leaders must balance the tension between these two forces, ensuring neither is neglected.

Managing Time, Resources, and Money

To balance these priorities effectively, you must become skilled at managing time, resources, and money. **Time management** is critical: you will need to carve out specific periods for focusing on your top projects without allowing the demands of core processes to overwhelm your schedule. This might involve delegating more of the day-to-day operations to trusted staff or volunteers, ensuring that you are not consumed by administrative work that could prevent you from giving your full attention to the year's most important initiatives. Creating a block schedule for yourself and your team is another important tool to use your time effectively. Make sure to include project time as well as 1:1 time with key people.

Resource management is another crucial skill. Each project and process will require people—paid staff and volunteers. Make sure you are allocating your most capable team members to the highest-priority projects and empowering them to lead and take ownership. Know who is best suited for each role and ensure that no single person is stretched too thin by trying to manage a critical project and the daily operations simultaneously.

Lastly, **financial management** plays a huge role in balancing core processes and projects. Some projects, like launching a new ministry or starting a capital campaign, will require significant financial resources. You must ensure that these initiatives are adequately funded without jeopardizing the budget allocated to maintaining your core operations. This will often involve making tough decisions about where to allocate funds and may require creative solutions like fundraising or reallocating existing resources. If your calendar and budget don't change, then you shouldn't say you've changed your priorities.

Prioritizing During Bottlenecks

There will inevitably be times when your parish experiences **bottlenecks**—when time, resources, or money become scarce, and decisions need to be made about what takes priority. In these moments, it is important to remain focused on the **mission and strategic vision**. When forced to choose, always ask: **Which effort will move us closer to fulfilling our mission?**

For example, if you are running into budget constraints and have to decide between funding a new ministry project or maintaining a current program, return to the goals set in your annual planning session. Which initiative will have a greater long-term impact on parish growth or engagement? Similarly, if you are short on staff or volunteer hours, you may need to temporarily deprioritize less critical tasks within core processes to free up resources for an essential project. The ability to make these difficult prioritization decisions in the face of constraints will define your effectiveness as a leader.

The Discipline to Stay on Track

One of the greatest challenges in balancing core processes and major projects is the **effort it takes to stay disciplined**. Distractions will come in many forms, often from well-meaning parishioners or unexpected opportunities that seem too good to pass up. It's easy to get pulled off track by someone proposing a new initiative or a minor crisis that demands your immediate attention.

Take, for example, the parishioner who approaches you after Mass with an idea for a new ministry they are passionate about. While their enthusiasm is genuine, and the idea may be worthwhile, you have to ask yourself whether this new ministry aligns with the **core priorities and projects** you've already committed to for the year. Does it support the mission, or would it pull resources and focus away from the key initiatives already in progress?

Here is where **discipline and discernment** play a crucial role. You must be able to say "no" to good ideas that are not the **right ideas for this year**. This is not about shutting down innovation or ignoring the desires of your parishioners; rather, it's about ensuring that the parish stays focused on what will have the most impact. At the same time, it's important to remain **attentive to the promptings of the Holy Spirit**. Sometimes, a new idea or unexpected challenge may be a call from God to pivot or reassess your priorities.

For instance, there may be moments when an unexpected event—a local crisis or a shift in community needs—requires you to reconsider your current focus. In these situations, **listening for the guidance of the Holy Spirit becomes essential.** You might find that an initiative you hadn't planned for should, in fact, take priority. In these moments, allow space for discernment, bringing your leadership team together in prayer and reflection before making decisions. Flexibility is important, but it should be grounded in spiritual wisdom, not reactive decision-making.

Distraction vs. Calling

Consider the scenario of a parish that has committed to a year-long project to build up their young adult ministry. Partway through the year, a well-meaning parishioner suggests building a youth center instead, arguing that this is an untapped area. While the idea is good, the parish has already allocated its resources to the young adults, which is part of the larger strategy to create healthy, vibrant families. In this case, the distraction could derail the focus and progress of the year's core projects. Staying disciplined means recognizing that **more isn't always better**, and saying "no" to new projects that don't align with the year's top priorities.

On the other hand, imagine a different scenario. The parish has been working on a capital campaign to fund the renovation of the church building. Midway through the campaign, the local community is hit with a natural disaster, leaving many parishioners displaced and in need of support. In this case, it may be necessary to shift focus, reallocating funds and resources to provide immediate assistance to those affected. While this wasn't part of the original plan, the parish recognizes the **call of the Holy Spirit** to respond to this urgent need, even if it means temporarily postponing the building project.

08

CHAPTER

Guiding Parish Growth:

Using Data to Evaluate
Progress and Drive Mission
Forward

In any parish, effective leadership requires more than just responding to daily challenges—it demands a clear vision of where the parish is headed and how well it's progressing toward its goals. Measuring progress may seem more at home in the world of business, but it is a critical tool in the Church as well. To lead a thriving parish, you must evaluate the practical and spiritual dimensions of your community. The challenge lies in balancing the need for measurable outcomes with the deeper, intangible work of spiritual growth and discipleship.

While it's true that "if you can't measure it, you can't manage it,"[1] it's equally important to remember that "numbers must serve the mission, not become the mission."[2] In the Church, measurable goals can offer clarity and direction, but they must always align with the broader spiritual purpose. It's not enough to focus solely on attendance or finances—true success is measured by how well we are living out the Gospel.

We will explore how to define success in the Church, why measurement matters, and how to apply it at the parish level and for individual spiritual growth. We'll look at how to use **scorecards** to track progress without losing sight of the mission. Finally, we'll discuss how to maintain the right balance between measurement and mission—ensuring that data guides your decisions without overshadowing your spiritual calling.

How Do We Define Success in the Church?

As a newly appointed pastor, or even as an experienced one, you might find yourself grappling with an essential question: **What does success mean in the Church?** It's a question that requires us to look deeper than the surface-level metrics we often associate with success in secular organizations—numbers like attendance, finances, and participation. In the context of parish life and ministry, success must be rooted in something far more profound: the spiritual transformation of individuals and the building of a community that reflects the love and teachings of Christ.

--- --- --- --- ---

1   Peter Drucker
2   W. Edwards Deming

Defining Success: A Spiritual Perspective

The word "success" comes from the Latin *succedere,* which means "to follow upon" or "to come after." In essence, success is achieved when our actions lead to the desired outcome. In ministry, the ultimate outcome is clear: the salvation of souls and leading people into deeper communion with God. However, this spiritual success cannot be directly measured in the way we track other objectives, like increasing donations or improving attendance. Instead, we must focus on more immediate and visible goals, primarily people's lives and actions aligning with the mission and the fruits of the Spirit. We'll talk more about this in the paragraphs that follow.

As pastors, our mission is tied directly to the mission of the Church, which Christ established to bring people to eternal life. Our success, then, should be measured by how effectively we lead people to encounter Christ, live out their faith, and grow in holiness. **Spiritual growth**—the transformation of hearts and minds to become disciples of Jesus—is the goal. But how do we assess such a deeply personal, spiritual process?

Signs of Success in Parish Life

While spiritual growth is difficult to quantify, there are visible signs that indicate whether a parish is thriving. The **sacraments**, for example, are clear markers of a parish's health. Increased participation in the sacraments can signify that parishioners are engaged in their faith, although we need other indicators to see if they are also seeking to deepen their relationship with God through these sacraments.

Other **tangible indicators** of success include:

▸ **Mass attendance**: Is the parish attracting people to worship regularly, or is attendance declining? Not only is Sunday attendance healthy, but how about daily Masses?

▸ **Volunteer engagement**: Are parishioners actively participating in ministries, outreach, and service? Are people getting burned out, or is good leadership succession occurring? Is there a strong sense of community?

▸ **Financial health**: Are donations and stewardship contributions stable or growing, allowing the parish to support its ministries and outreach efforts?

▸ **Ministry vitality**: Are the various ministries within the parish vibrant and growing, meeting the spiritual needs of different demographics—youth, families, seniors, and marginalized communities?

These indicators, while measurable, should not be viewed as the **ultimate goals**. Rather, they are signposts pointing to deeper spiritual realities: **the transformation of lives and hearts**. A parish may have growing numbers in attendance, but if parishioners are not experiencing spiritual growth, then the parish is falling short of its true mission.

A Reminder on the Role of Numbers

As discussed earlier in this book, numbers are incredibly useful, but their true value lies in helping us identify where there may be a problem in the behavior of a system, process, technology or person—not in managing the numbers themselves or, worse, objectifying the people behind those numbers. Misapplying metrics can lead to focusing on the wrong goals and even objectifying people. We must always remember that numbers should guide our mission, not replace the heart of it.

Recall earlier the example of a person with a fever: when someone goes to the hospital with a high temperature, the medical team measures their vital signs: body temperature, heart rate, blood pressure, and oxygen levels. These numbers are crucial for diagnosing that something is wrong, but they aren't the problem in and of themselves. The fever is a symptom pointing to something deeper, such as an infection or an underlying health issue.

Success as a Journey of Spiritual Growth

The Bible provides a helpful framework for understanding success in the Church. James 2:26 reminds us, "Faith without works is dead." True success in ministry involves an **inner conversion** of the heart and **outward actions** that reflect that transformation. While outward signs like attendance and participation are important, they must be accompanied by the deeper work of helping individuals grow in faith and love of God.

Jesus frequently emphasized the need for inner transformation over external appearances. In Matthew 23:27, He calls out the Pharisees as "whitewashed tombs," clean on the outside but spiritually dead inside. This is a reminder to pastors that success isn't about creating a parish that looks perfect from the outside but rather about nurturing the inner lives of parishioners, leading them to become true disciples of Christ.

Success in the Church, then, is best understood as a **journey of spiritual growth**. It begins with evangelization, where individuals are introduced to the faith and the person of Jesus Christ and ultimately become his disciples. It continues through formation, where they grow in understanding, holiness, and the practice of their faith. Finally, it leads to **mission**, where individuals are empowered to live out their faith in the world and bring others to Christ.

The Importance of Defining Success

It's critical for pastors to define success clearly, not only for themselves but also for their teams. One common issue in parishes and other organizations is the lack of clarity around what success looks like. Imagine a parish staff meeting where each person is diligently working on various tasks but lacks a unified understanding of what success entails. In this scenario, even well-intentioned efforts may be misaligned, leading to frustration and confusion. Parish leaders need to articulate a **vision of success** that everyone understands, so each ministry and individual knows how their work fits into the broader mission.

Why Measure Things in the Church?

As a pastor, you might feel a certain hesitation about measuring success in your parish. After all, isn't our work spiritual in nature? Shouldn't we simply trust in God's plan and leave the results to Him? You may have heard someone say, or even thought yourself, "Well, I just plant the seeds and let the Spirit produce the fruit, so measuring isn't trusting God to do His part." This perspective, while well-intentioned, overlooks an important aspect of our role as stewards of God's gifts.

Consider the parable of the talents in Matthew 25. The master says to the faithful servant,

> *"Well done, my good and faithful servant. Since you were faithful in small matters, I will give you great responsibilities."*
>
> **MATTHEW 25:23**

This parable teaches us that God expects us to actively use the gifts and opportunities He provides. The master praises the servants who worked to increase what was entrusted to them and condemns the one who did nothing. Human effort and responsible stewardship are not only expected but valued by God.

So while it's true that we must trust God to produce spiritual growth because all grace comes from God through Jesus Christ, Scripture also emphasizes our responsibility to be active stewards of what God entrusts to us. Measuring progress is not a lack of faith but an expression of responsible stewardship, ensuring that we are faithfully using our gifts and opportunities in alignment with God's purposes.

Another biblical example that supports the idea of measurement and evaluation is found in Luke 13:8-9. In this parable, a man had a fig tree planted in his vineyard. For three years, he came seeking fruit but found none. He then told the gardener to cut it down, but the gardener replied, "Sir, leave it for this year also, and I shall cultivate the ground around it and fertilize it; it may bear fruit in the future. If not, you can cut it down." This parable highlights God's patience, giving the tree another chance to bear fruit. However, it also underscores the necessity of human effort—cultivating and fertilizing the tree to encourage growth.

As stewards of resources, we have a responsibility to be diligent in how we spend our time, money, and energy. Measurement helps us ensure that we're using these resources effectively in service of our mission. It allows us to identify areas where we're bearing fruit and areas where we might need to "cultivate and fertilize" more intentionally.

However, it's crucial to approach measurement with wisdom and discernment. You never want to fall into the trap of measuring the wrong things or letting the measurement become the target (a phenomenon known as Goodhart's Law). Driving solely for higher numbers can lead to lots of activity but little conversion of heart. Focusing exclusively on social media likes, better reviews on Google, higher attendance numbers, or increased revenue can lead to superficial gains without deep spiritual growth. Even measuring good things, like vocations and fundraising, if they come to define success, can distract us from the more important work of moving people closer to Jesus.

The ultimate sign of success for a parish is to create apostles, sometimes called missionary disciples, just as Jesus did. Our measurements should reflect this goal, helping us to gauge how effectively we're leading people through the stages of spiritual growth—from initial evangelization, through deeper formation, to becoming active disciples who share their faith with others.

What to Measure in the Church?

As you settle into your role as a new pastor, you might be wondering what exactly you should be measuring to gauge the health and effectiveness of your parish. The answer will vary depending on where your parish is in its life cycle and how it's adapting to the current societal situation. However, there are some key areas that every parish should consider tracking.

Let's start with the basics that most parishes already measure:

1. **Finances:** This includes money coming in, money going out, savings, debt, and the ratio of online giving to envelope or basket donations. While a thorough review of all financial reports is important, these basic metrics provide a quick snapshot of your parish's financial health.

2. **Attendance:** Mass numbers are typically measured two to four times a year on average Sundays (not holidays or during summer breaks). While you may have a list of registered parishioners, these lists are often not well-maintained and may not accurately reflect active participation. Regular Mass attendance is usually a more reliable indicator of parish engagement.

3. **Ministries:** Create a comprehensive list of all ministries, including the number of volunteers, who's in charge (with contact information), and an assessment of how well each ministry serves the needs of the Church.

These basic metrics provide a foundation, but to truly understand the spiritual health of your parish, you'll want to dig deeper. More diligent parishes often track:

- **Sacramental participation:** Numbers for baptisms, weddings, first communions, confirmations, and anointings. Some even count confessions, which can be a great indicator of spiritual growth.
- **Faith formation:** Participation in religious education programs for both children and adults.
- **Vocations:** While rare, any ordinations or entries into religious life are certainly worth celebrating and tracking! Holy marriages are also vocations.

Parishes that are more advanced in their approach to measurement might also look at:

- **Daily Mass attendance**
- **Small group participation**
- **Adoration participants**
- **Number of spiritual directors or mentors**
- **Retreat attendance**

Again, remember that our goal is not just participation but transformation. A parish that is fully on mission will strive to understand where people are in their spiritual journey. This means tracking how many parishioners are at various stages of faith development, from initial curiosity about the faith, through active engagement, to becoming missionary disciples themselves.

By understanding where your parishioners are in this journey, you can tailor your ministry efforts more effectively and track true spiritual growth over time.

Measuring Individual Team Members: A Path to Personal Accountability and Growth

In a parish setting, the success of individual team members is deeply connected to the success of the parish as a whole. To keep the parish on mission, each team member—whether staff, volunteer, or ministry leader—needs to have a clear understanding of their role and how it contributes to the parish's goals. To do this effectively, every team member should have a defined set of **priorities** that relate to either the parish's **core processes**, **key projects**, or both. These priorities give them a clear sense of purpose and enable them to measure their own success each day.

Defining Clear Priorities: Processes and Projects

Every individual in your parish, whether they are running ministries or supporting the business operations of the parish, is working within the context of **processes** or **projects**. It's essential to clearly define what these are for each team member.

▸ **Processes** are the ongoing, routine tasks that keep the parish functioning smoothly. These include responsibilities like preparing for Mass, managing finances, overseeing communications, or coordinating volunteer teams.

▸ **Projects** are specific, time-bound initiatives that have a clear start and end, such as organizing a parish retreat, launching a new ministry, or overseeing a capital campaign.

For each individual, the balance between process work and project work will vary. Some team members, such as administrative staff, may spend most of their time ensuring processes run smoothly, while others, like a youth minister, may be heavily involved in planning and executing projects such as events or new groups. In either case, success comes from having **well-defined priorities** related to their specific responsibilities.

Measurable Success: Daily Accountability

The key takeaway for measuring individual success is that each team member should know, on any given day, how well they are doing. This is achieved by having **measurable priorities** that allow for daily reflection on progress. Just as the parish has larger, measurable goals, each person should be able to evaluate their own performance in real-time based on clear criteria.

For example, consider a parish business manager whose responsibilities revolve around financial processes. Their list of measurable priorities might include:

- ▸ **Timely processing of invoices and payroll** (process)
- ▸ **Ensuring monthly financial reports are accurate and on time** (process)
- ▸ **Coordinating the annual stewardship campaign** (project)

On any given day, the business manager can measure their success by asking: Did I complete my daily financial tasks? Did I stay on track with the stewardship campaign timeline? These simple questions provide immediate feedback and accountability.

For someone overseeing a project, like organizing a parish-wide retreat, their priorities might look like this:

- ▸ **Recruiting and coordinating a retreat planning team** (process)
- ▸ **Securing a venue and scheduling speakers by a set deadline** (project)
- ▸ **Ensuring the event communication plan is in place and implemented** (project)

Each day, the retreat organizer can measure their progress by reflecting on key tasks: Did I connect with the team? Did I finalize the speaker schedule? Is the event being promoted effectively? These priorities keep the team member focused and accountable, providing a sense of daily accomplishment.

Making Success Measurable

For every team member, the process of measuring success should be straightforward and empowering. Here are a few guidelines to ensure that each individual can measure their success every day:

1. **Tie daily tasks to larger priorities**: Help team members see the connection between their daily responsibilities and the overall goals of the parish. Every action should contribute to either advancing a project or maintaining a core process.

2. **Set clear, measurable outcomes**: For each responsibility, there should be a clear, measurable goal. This could be a daily checklist for processes (e.g., complete this task by a specific time) or a timeline for project milestones (e.g., achieve this step by the end of the week).

3. **Ensure alignment with parish goals**: Each person's priorities should align with the broader parish objectives set during the annual planning process. If the parish's goal is to improve outreach, for example, every team member involved in ministry should have priorities that directly contribute to that effort.

4. **Provide regular feedback and check-ins**: Regular check-ins with the pastor or leadership team provide an opportunity to discuss progress, offer feedback, and make adjustments. These conversations can help team members stay focused on what's most important while also feeling supported in their work.

Empowering Team Members for Success

Ultimately, the goal of measuring individual team members is not just about tracking tasks—it's about **empowerment**. When people know what is expected of them and how to measure their own success, they are more motivated, focused, and capable of contributing to the mission of the parish. A clear list of priorities gives each person the ability to take ownership of their work and confidently evaluate their progress.

By providing team members with **measurable, daily priorities**, you're not just ensuring that tasks get done—you're helping them grow as leaders and disciples, enabling them to see how their work directly supports the parish's mission and its broader spiritual goals. This sense of purpose and accountability is crucial for building a strong, mission-driven team that is efficient and deeply committed to the Church's work.

Scorecards: A Tool for Clarity, Accountability, and Mission Alignment

A **scorecard** is a simple yet powerful tool that helps parish leaders track progress, stay aligned with priorities, and make informed decisions. It serves as a visual dashboard for the key metrics that matter most in both operational and spiritual aspects of parish life. By using a scorecard, you can easily see how well your parish is progressing toward its goals, identify areas that need improvement, and ensure that everyone on the team is accountable for their responsibilities.

Why Use Scorecards?

Scorecards bring structure to the often complex and multifaceted operations of a parish. They are important for several reasons:

1. **Clarity**: Scorecards provide a clear picture of where the parish stands in relation to its goals. Rather than relying on vague perceptions of success or failure, you can see concrete data that highlights the strengths and weaknesses in your operations. This clarity helps in making decisions and focusing efforts where they are most needed.

2. **Accountability**: With a scorecard, there is a built-in mechanism for holding individuals and teams accountable. When key metrics are regularly reviewed, it becomes clear whether specific areas are performing well or falling behind. This accountability is essential for maintaining momentum and ensuring that the parish continues to move toward its mission.

3. **Alignment with mission**: A scorecard helps keep the focus on what matters most—your parish's mission. By tracking progress in critical areas, you can ensure that the parish's day-to-day operations and projects align with its broader spiritual and organizational goals. This helps prevent distractions and ensures that the work being done is always contributing to the mission.

4. **Informed decision-making**: Instead of making decisions based on intuition or assumptions, a scorecard provides data to inform leadership choices. This enables more strategic planning and resource allocation, ensuring that the parish invests time and energy where it will have the greatest impact.

What to Include in a Scorecard

A well-designed scorecard tracks the **key performance indicators (KPIs)** that are most important for your parish's health and mission. While every parish is different, a typical scorecard might include metrics that cover **processes** (the ongoing functions of parish life) and **projects** (the time-bound initiatives).

Here are some areas you might include in your parish scorecard:

▸ **Mass attendance**: Track the weekly and monthly attendance numbers at Mass. This helps you see whether more people are engaging in worship, especially after specific efforts like outreach or new ministries.

▸ **Sacramental participation**: Include metrics such as baptisms, confirmations, marriages, and confessions. These are tangible signs of parishioner engagement in the faith and sacramental life of the Church.

▸ **Financial health**: Track key financial indicators, such as weekly offertory, contributions to capital campaigns, and stewardship donations. Financial health is essential for sustaining ministries and operations.

▸ **Volunteer engagement**: Measure the number of active volunteers and the hours they contribute. High volunteer engagement is a sign of a vibrant parish community, while a drop in participation could signal a need for renewed efforts in recruitment or support.

▸ **Key projects**: Include metrics for the progress of top parish projects. For example, if you are launching a new ministry or renovating parish facilities, track milestones to ensure the project stays on time and within budget.

▸ **Ministry engagement**: Track participation in ministries such as OCIA, Bible studies, youth groups, and social outreach programs. This shows whether parishioners are growing in their faith and connecting with the parish's mission in deeper ways.

Each metric should have a clear **target** you're aiming for, whether it's a specific number, percentage increase, or completion of a project milestone.

How to Use Scorecards

Once you've decided what to include in your scorecard, it's important to establish a rhythm for reviewing and using it. Here's a step-by-step approach to getting the most out of your scorecard:

1. **Create and customize**: Start by selecting the metrics that align with your parish's unique goals and mission. Ensure that each item on the scorecard can be clearly measured, whether through attendance figures, financial reports, or project milestones.

2. **Set regular review meetings**: A scorecard is most effective when it is reviewed consistently. Schedule regular meetings—monthly or quarterly—where the leadership team can review the scorecard together. These meetings are an opportunity to assess whether the parish is on track and to discuss any areas that need attention.

3. **Monitor progress**: During each review, compare the current numbers to your targets. Are you meeting your goals for the month? If not, what obstacles are preventing progress, and how can they be addressed? Regularly monitoring progress allows you to spot issues early and adjust course if needed.

4. **Hold teams accountable**: Each section of the scorecard should have an individual or team responsible for it. During your review meetings, ask those responsible for specific areas to provide updates on their progress and any challenges they are facing. This level of accountability ensures that everyone is actively working toward the parish's goals.

5. **Celebrate successes**: A scorecard isn't just a tool for pointing out problems—it's also an opportunity to celebrate what's going well. When you see positive movement on the scorecard, take time to acknowledge the hard work and achievements of your team. Celebrating small wins boosts morale and encourages continued effort.

6. **Adjust as needed**: As the year progresses, you may need to adjust your targets based on new insights or changing circumstances. For example, if your parish experiences unexpected growth, you may want to set more ambitious attendance or financial targets. Alternatively, if a project faces delays, you might adjust timelines and expectations.

Keeping Scorecards Mission-Focused

While scorecards are highly effective for tracking progress, their purpose is to **serve the mission**, not replace it. If your scorecard shows that attendance is declining, for example, the solution isn't just to push for more people in the pews—it's to ask deeper questions about whether parishioners are feeling spiritually fed and engaged.

In this way, a scorecard is a **diagnostic tool**, much like how a doctor uses vital signs to assess a patient's health. The numbers help reveal what's going well and what needs attention.

Balancing Measurement with Mission: A Reminder to Keep Focused on What Matters

Numbers are your guideposts. They tell you when and where to look, but they will never replace the heart of your parish's mission. **Spiritual growth, community transformation, and faith-filled discipleship**—these are your true measures of success. The data will help you stay on track, but it is your discernment, leadership, and commitment to the mission that will ultimately determine how well your parish fulfills its call to bring people into a deeper relationship with Christ.

09

CHAPTER

Problem Solving:

Making Decisions
& Conflict Management

L eading a parish inevitably involves navigating a wide range of challenges, from logistical issues to interpersonal conflicts, all while ensuring the Church's mission remains at the forefront. Problem-solving, then, becomes one of the most important tools in your leadership toolbox. It's not just about finding solutions to immediate problems but about adopting a structured approach to identify root causes, resolve issues efficiently, and guide your parish through necessary changes in a way that aligns with your mission.

In this chapter, we will explore how to **scope an issue** properly, giving you the clarity needed to define what needs to be addressed. You will also learn a **clear process for resolving issues**, from gathering facts to identifying possible solutions and implementing them effectively. Beyond problem-solving, you will gain insights into **managing change** in your organization—a critical skill as even the best solutions often require transitions that impact your staff, volunteers, and parishioners. Finally, we will discuss **healthy conflict management**, ensuring that differing perspectives lead to growth and collaboration rather than division.

Scoping an Issue

"Scoping" a problem is the critical first step in effective problem-solving. Without a clear understanding of the issue at hand, any attempt to resolve it can lead to wasted resources, misaligned solutions, and frustration for everyone involved. By fully scoping the issue, you ensure that you're addressing the real problem—not just the symptoms. Scoping involves breaking down the problem, analyzing its root causes, assessing timing, and understanding all the facts, assumptions, opinions, and feelings surrounding it. Here's how to do it effectively:

1. Clear Summary of the Problem or Decision

The first step is to **define the core problem** in a clear and concise way. This is not the time for vague or overly broad statements. Instead, get specific about what the issue is and why it matters.

What is the core issue? For example, is it a drop in Mass attendance, a gap in communication between staff members, or a financial shortfall?

Why is it important? What are the potential impacts if the problem isn't addressed? For instance, a drop in attendance could mean fewer people receiving the sacraments, lower engagement in parish activities, and reduced stewardship.

Who is affected? Identify the key stakeholders who are directly impacted by the issue—parishioners, staff, volunteers, or even the wider community. This will help you understand the broader implications of the problem.

A well-defined problem sets the stage for finding an effective solution. A clear summary might look like this:

"We are experiencing a 20% decline in Mass attendance over the past six months, which could impact our ability to fulfill the parish mission of spiritual growth and community engagement. Parishioners and ministry leaders are concerned about the reduced participation, and our stewardship contributions have declined as a result."

2. Root Cause Analysis

Once you have clearly defined the problem, the next step is to identify the **root cause**. Often, what we perceive as the problem is merely a symptom of something deeper. For example, a decline in attendance might be the result of changing demographics, dissatisfaction with the liturgy, or a lack of engagement in parish ministries.

A useful method to uncover the root cause is the **5 Whys Technique**. Ask "why" repeatedly until you get to the underlying reason behind the issue. For example:

Why is Mass attendance declining? (The community isn't as engaged as before.)

Why aren't they engaged? (The current programs aren't meeting their spiritual needs.)

Why aren't the programs meeting their needs? (We haven't updated our ministries or surveyed parishioners in years.)

Why haven't we surveyed parishioners? (We assumed past attendance trends would continue.)

Why did we assume that? (We didn't account for changes in the community's demographics or needs.)

By the end of this process, you should have a clearer understanding of the root cause and be in a better position to address it. Keep in mind that sometimes we might not have the data needed to know what the root cause is.

3. Is Now the Time for Resolution?

Not every problem requires immediate resolution. It's important to assess whether now is the right time to act or if you need more information or resources before proceeding.

Urgency: Is this a problem that requires an immediate solution, or can it wait? For example, a structural issue in your building might require immediate action, while updating your parish's website could be a longer-term project.

Resources: Do you have the people, time, and financial resources to tackle this issue now? If not, you might need to delay resolution or break the problem down into smaller, more manageable steps.

Consequences of delay: What happens if you don't address the issue now? Will it worsen over time, or are the risks of waiting low?

Sometimes, taking the time to gather more data or build a stronger team can lead to a more effective resolution.

4. Distinguishing Between Facts, Assumptions, Opinions, and Feelings

When scoping an issue, it's crucial to separate **facts** from **assumptions, opinions, and feelings**. All of these play a role in problem-solving, but they need to be treated differently.

Facts: These are objective pieces of information. For example, a fact might be "Mass attendance has declined by 20% over the last six months."

Assumptions: These are beliefs you hold without solid evidence. For example, assuming that people aren't attending because they don't like the new music style is an assumption. This needs to be tested or validated before acting on it.

Opinions: Opinions are subjective judgments, such as "I think the liturgy has become less engaging." While valid, they are not the same as facts and should be weighed accordingly.

Feelings: Emotional responses, such as "I feel discouraged by the lack of participation," are important to acknowledge but should not drive the decision-making process. Emotions often provide clues about deeper issues but should be examined alongside the facts.

Clearly distinguishing between these elements allows you to build a more accurate picture of the situation and prevents assumptions or feelings from clouding judgment.

5. Exploring Possible Solutions

After scoping the issue and analyzing its root cause, you can move on to generating **possible solutions**. At this stage, you're brainstorming ideas, so don't limit yourself— think creatively about how to address the problem.

Brainstorming: Gather ideas from key stakeholders, including staff, volunteers, and parishioners. This helps ensure that you consider different perspectives and potential solutions.

Short-term vs. long-term solutions: Some solutions may address the problem quickly, while others may take longer but provide a more sustainable fix. For instance, a quick fix for declining attendance might be a special outreach event, while a longer-term solution could involve restructuring ministries to better meet parishioner needs.

Pros and cons: Evaluate the advantages and disadvantages of each potential solution. For example, one solution might increase engagement but strain resources, while another might be more cost-effective but less impactful.

At this point, it's important to weigh the pros and cons to ensure that the solution aligns with the parish's mission and resources.

6. Impact on Stakeholders and Unintended Consequences

Consider how each potential solution will affect the various stakeholders in your parish. Every solution has ripple effects, and you must anticipate and plan for them.

Stakeholder impact: How will staff, volunteers, parishioners, or ministry leaders be affected by the change? Will they need additional support or training?

Unintended consequences: What potential negative outcomes could arise from your chosen solution? For instance, restructuring ministries to engage more parishioners could inadvertently alienate long-standing volunteers who are resistant to change.

Thinking through these consequences can help prevent new problems from arising and ensure that your solution is sustainable.

7. Timing and Feasibility

Lastly, ensure that the solution you choose can be implemented within the necessary timeframe and with the available resources.

Timing: Consider the best time to implement the solution. For example, launching a new program during Lent might generate more engagement, while the summer months might be less ideal due to lower attendance.

Feasibility: Does your parish have the budget, personnel, and support needed to implement the solution? If not, is there a way to phase the solution in gradually?

By carefully scoping the issue, identifying root causes, and evaluating solutions with these considerations in mind, you can ensure that the problem-solving process is thoughtful and effective.

A Clear Process for Resolving Issues

Effective leadership in a parish requires not only the ability to identify problems but also a structured process for resolving them. Whether the issue is operational, strategic, or relational, having a clear framework in place ensures that challenges are addressed efficiently and in alignment with the parish's mission. This process begins with defining the problem and leads all the way through to action, emphasizing clarity, accountability, and the use of discernment.

1. Define the Problem

The first step in resolving any issue is to **clearly define the problem**. Vague or poorly understood issues often lead to misguided solutions, so it's crucial to start with a clear understanding of what you're addressing.

- **Summarize the issue**: Clearly state the problem, who it affects, and why it matters.
- **Decide on involvement**: Determine whether the problem requires input from the full leadership team or if it can be resolved by an individual leader or smaller group.

  - **Involve your leadership team** when the issue affects multiple ministries or stakeholders, or when diverse perspectives are needed.
  - **Resolve as a leader** for more straightforward, operational matters, either by making the decision yourself or delegating it to the appropriate person.

2. Subsidiarity: Decision at the Lowest Level

One of the most effective management principles is **subsidiarity**, which encourages decisions to be made at the **lowest appropriate level**. This empowers team members, improves efficiency, and builds a culture of trust and accountability.

As a leader, your role is to **oversee** and ensure decisions align with the parish's mission and broader goals rather than micromanaging.

Empower decision-making: Let the team closest to the problem own the decision, as they often have the most context.

Oversight and alignment: Guide decisions to ensure they fit with the parish's broader mission but resist the urge to intervene unless necessary.

Escalation: Ensure that there is a clear path to escalate decisions if they become too complex or require wider input, but otherwise, trust your team to handle their responsibilities.

3. Using Ignatian Discernment

For **mission-critical decisions** or those that deeply affect the spiritual life of the parish, it's important to incorporate **Ignatian discernment**—a process rooted in prayerful reflection, weighing options, and seeking the greater good.

This approach, grounded in centuries of wisdom, encourages you and your team to reflect on how each decision serves God's mission. It's a blend of spiritual reflection and practical judgment that goes beyond data-driven decision-making.

Take time for discernment: When facing significant decisions, model a thoughtful approach by taking time for prayer and reflection. Encourage your team to do the same. A detailed guide to Ignatian discernment is included in the workbook accompanying this text, providing steps for integrating these principles into your decision-making process.

4. Avoid Relitigating Issues

Once a decision has been made, commit to it. Reopening decisions without new, significant information leads to confusion, delays, and frustration.

No relitigating: Once a decision is reached, make it clear that it should not be revisited unless there is new, important information. Make sure you document decisions in your project management tool, in your SOPs, as well as in your meeting notes.

New information threshold: If new data emerges, assess whether it truly requires revisiting the decision. Resist the urge to reopen issues due to second-guessing or discomfort with the change.

5. Accepting Imperfection in Decision-Making

In leadership, you'll rarely have perfect or complete information when making decisions. Waiting for perfect clarity can lead to paralysis, so it's critical to strike a balance between **data and discernment**.

Acknowledge imperfection: Understand that every decision involves some degree of uncertainty. Gather as much information as possible but recognize when it's time to act.

Commit to action: Once a decision is made, fully commit to it. Don't delay or hesitate while waiting for additional data that may never materialize.

6. Turn Decisions into Action Items

One of the most critical steps in any decision-making process is translating that decision into **specific, actionable tasks**. A decision without a clear follow-up plan is unlikely to lead to meaningful change. This is where the concept of **"Next Step, Due Date, and Responsible Party"** becomes essential.

▸▸ **Break down decisions into manageable steps**: Every decision should result in concrete next steps that can be completed within **a week**. Tasks that are too large tend to stall progress, so breaking them down ensures that forward momentum is maintained.

>   ▸▸ For example, instead of saying, "Improve outreach," break it down into, "Draft the outreach plan by Friday."

▸▸ **Next Step, Due Date, Responsible Party**: Every action item must be clearly assigned using this framework. It's one of the most powerful management tools available. Knowing exactly who is responsible for a task, when it's due, and what the next step is keeps the team accountable and on track.

▸ **Delegate effectively**: Ensure that tasks are assigned based on capability and availability. Make sure the person responsible for each task understands their role and has the resources they need.

7. Set Due Dates

Clear deadlines are vital to maintaining progress. Without them, tasks can drift, leading to delays and missed opportunities.

Specific due dates: Avoid vague timelines like "next week" or "soon." Use concrete deadlines such as "By Tuesday, September 19" to ensure accountability.

Track progress: Use project management tools, weekly meetings, or checklists to monitor the completion of tasks. This keeps everyone accountable and ensures nothing slips through the cracks.

8. Follow-Up and Review

After action steps are initiated, it's important to have a system of **regular check-ins**. These meetings ensure that progress is being made, allow for adjustments, and help celebrate wins along the way.

Weekly or biweekly check-ins: These regular reviews help to maintain momentum and ensure tasks are being completed on time.

Celebrate small wins: Acknowledge progress by celebrating milestones, no matter how small. This helps keep the team motivated and reinforces a sense of accomplishment.

Adjust as needed: Be flexible in your approach. If something isn't working, adjust the plan while still holding individuals accountable for their responsibilities.

9. Closure and Reflection

Once the issue is resolved and all action items are completed, it's important to bring closure to the process. This involves reflecting on the effectiveness of the solution and documenting the lessons learned.

Evaluate the outcome: After the resolution, take time to reflect on whether the solution worked. Did it solve the problem effectively? What impact did it have on the parish?

Lessons learned: Reflect on what worked well and what could be improved for future issues.

Document the process: Ensure that the entire decision-making process is documented. This helps inform future decisions and serves as a valuable resource for similar challenges down the road.

Managing Conflict in a Parish Setting

Conflict itself is not inherently bad; in fact, when managed effectively, it can lead to growth, better understanding, and improved outcomes. When conflict is left unresolved or is mishandled, it can undermine relationships, disrupt the parish's mission, and damage the community.

Understanding how to identify, address, and manage conflict in a healthy way is an essential skill for parish leaders.

What is Conflict?

At its core, conflict arises from differences. These differences can manifest in three key areas:

1. **Values:** Conflicts arise when individuals or groups hold different values. For example, some parishioners may prioritize tradition in worship, while others may value innovation and modernization. These value-based conflicts can be deeply personal and challenging to resolve.
2. **Goals:** Conflicts can also stem from differences in goals. One ministry may be focused on increasing social outreach, while another prioritizes internal spiritual formation. If both ministries are competing for the same resources or attention, this misalignment of goals can create tension.
3. **Style:** Finally, differences in personal styles can lead to conflict. Some people may have a direct, task-oriented communication style,

while others prefer a more relational, consensus-building approach. Misunderstandings and frustrations can arise when people don't see eye to eye on how things should get done.

Conflicts can often involve more than one of these areas. For instance, a disagreement over how to run a parish event might stem from different goals (such as whether the focus should be on fundraising or community-building), as well as different styles (such as a preference for formal vs. informal approaches). Additionally, conflicts over resources like money aren't usually about the money itself but about differing values, goals, or styles in how to handle money. This applies not just to personal relationships but also to conflicts within parishes, organizations, or even nations.

Recognizing which of these areas a conflict stems from—and that it may involve more than one area—is the first step in addressing it effectively.

Why is Managing Conflict Important?

Unresolved or poorly managed conflict can damage relationships and weaken the fabric of the parish community. It can:

Undermine trust: People may lose faith in leadership or each other if they feel their concerns aren't being heard or resolved.

Distract from the mission: Conflict can consume time and energy that should be spent on fulfilling the parish's mission. Left unchecked, it can shift focus away from ministry and service.

Create division: Without resolution, conflicts can grow into larger divisions, splintering the community and harming the sense of unity within the parish.

However, when conflict is managed well, it can:

Promote growth: Healthy conflict encourages open dialogue, leading to better understanding and innovative solutions.

Strengthen relationships: Resolving conflict respectfully and constructively can deepen trust and strengthen bonds within the community.

Clarify goals: Addressing conflict can help bring misaligned goals or values into alignment, ensuring the parish is moving in a unified direction.

Healthy vs. Unhealthy Conflict

Healthy conflict involves open, respectful communication where differing viewpoints are expressed and listened to in a constructive manner. In healthy conflict:

- People feel safe to express their concerns.
- Disagreements are focused on ideas, goals, or styles—not personal attacks.
- The resolution process is collaborative, with everyone working toward a mutually beneficial outcome.
- Emotions are acknowledged but not allowed to dominate or derail the discussion.

Unhealthy conflict, on the other hand, is marked by:

- Personal attacks or blaming
- Avoidance of the issue, leading to simmering resentment or passive-aggressive behavior
- Power struggles or competition, where individuals are more focused on "winning" than finding a solution
- Emotional outbursts that derail the conversation or lead to hurt feelings

A key skill for parish leaders is identifying whether a conflict is being handled in a healthy or unhealthy way. If the conflict is devolving into personal attacks, stonewalling, or emotional escalation, it's a sign that the situation needs intervention.

When to Get Involved

As a leader, it's important to know when to step in and manage conflict and when to let it play out naturally. Here are some guidelines to help you determine when to get involved:

Get involved when the conflict is disrupting the parish's mission: If the conflict is preventing the parish from functioning effectively—whether it's impacting ministries, staff productivity, or the spiritual health of the community—it's time to step in.

Intervene if the conflict is becoming personal or hostile: If disagreements are escalating into personal attacks or creating a hostile environment, leadership intervention is necessary to restore a sense of respect and civility.

Step in when there is a power imbalance: If one party in the conflict has significantly more influence or authority than the other, you may need to step in to ensure that the less powerful individual or group is heard and treated fairly.

Let it play out when it's a difference of opinion: If the conflict is a healthy exchange of ideas or goals and both parties are engaging respectfully, it's often best to let the conversation unfold naturally. Conflict can be a creative and necessary force for innovation and growth.

Monitor but don't intervene immediately: In situations where the conflict is mild and not yet disruptive, it can be helpful to monitor the situation before stepping in. Sometimes, people can resolve their differences without leadership intervention. If you solve everyone's conflicts, you're teaching them to always come to you.

How to Manage Conflict Effectively

Managing conflict well requires a mix of skills: communication, emotional intelligence, and discernment. Here's how to navigate conflict in a parish setting:

1. **Listen actively and empathetically.**

   ▸ The first step in resolving conflict is to truly listen to all parties involved. Make sure each person feels heard and respected. Reflect back what you're hearing to ensure understanding and show empathy.

   ▸ Avoid interrupting or making assumptions. Let each party explain their perspective fully before jumping in with solutions.

2. **Stay focused on the issue, not the person.**

    ▸ When addressing conflict, keep the conversation centered on the disagreement—whether it's about values, goals, or styles. Avoid letting the conversation devolve into personal criticism or blame.

    ▸ Frame the conflict in terms of the issue at hand and how resolving it will help move the parish forward.

3. **Acknowledge emotions but don't let them take over.**

    ▸ Emotions are a natural part of conflict, and it's important to acknowledge them. However, make sure that emotions don't dominate the conversation. Encourage people to express their feelings, but guide them toward productive dialogue.

    ▸ Be aware of your own emotions as a leader. Stay calm, composed, and objective, modeling the behavior you expect from others.

4. **Seek common ground.**

    ▸ Even in the midst of conflict, there's often common ground that both parties can agree on. Whether it's shared values or a mutual desire to serve the parish, identifying common ground can help defuse tension and create a path forward.

    ▸ Focus on the bigger picture: the parish's mission and the work of the Church. Remind everyone that, despite their differences, they are working toward the same overall goal.

5. **Facilitate problem-solving.**

    ▸ Once the issues have been aired and emotions have been acknowledged, guide the group toward finding a solution. Encourage a collaborative approach to problem-solving, where each person's input is valued.

    ▸ Be prepared to mediate if the conversation gets stuck or if the conflict is too heated for the parties to resolve on their own.

6. **Follow through and check-in.**

» After a resolution has been reached, follow up with the parties involved to ensure that the conflict has truly been resolved and that no lingering resentment remains.

» Regular check-ins can help prevent the same issues from resurfacing and ensure that the resolution is lasting.

Conclusion

Conflict is a natural and necessary part of parish life. When handled well, it can lead to growth, stronger relationships, and clearer goals. As a parish leader, your role is not to avoid conflict but to manage it in a way that keeps the focus on the mission, fosters healthy dialogue, and resolves differences constructively. By understanding the causes of conflict—whether they stem from values, goals, or styles—and using a structured approach to address it, you can ensure that disagreements don't divide your community but rather strengthen it.

10

CHAPTER

Alignment

Effective parish leadership is about more than just managing operations; it's about creating alignment across every level of your organization so that everyone is moving in the same direction, united by a common mission. This chapter will guide you through the key practices that bring your team together, ensuring clarity, efficiency, and purpose.

You will learn how to run effective meetings that keep your team focused and productive, and you'll discover the power of the daily huddle to enhance communication and keep everyone aligned on immediate priorities. We'll also dive into how to choose our Parish Approach, a model for decision-making that helps establish consistency in how the parish operates—whether it's selecting technology platforms or creating workflows—while leaving room for flexibility. Finally, we'll explore practical strategies for aligning the organization, ensuring that all efforts are coordinated and aimed at fulfilling the parish's mission.

The Importance of a Weekly Meeting Rhythm

Consistency is key to keeping a parish team aligned and focused on its mission. Establishing a **weekly meeting rhythm** helps create a predictable structure for communication and ensures that important topics are addressed regularly. Here's a suggested rhythm for keeping your team in sync:

1. Weekly Leadership Meetings:

Once a week, the leadership team should meet for 60 to 90 minutes to discuss parish strategy, progress on key initiatives, and any critical issues that need to be addressed. These meetings focus on high-level decision-making, reviewing key metrics, and planning for the future.

These meetings are essential for long-term alignment and should cover strategic goals, review of the parish scorecard, and major projects.

2. Daily Huddles:

These quick, daily stand-ups help keep everyone on the same page for day-to-day tasks. They prevent small issues from becoming big problems and keep the team accountable for making progress every day.

The huddle keeps communication flowing and ensures that no one is working in isolation. It also highlights any blockers that need to be addressed before they slow down progress.

3.   **1:1 Meetings (twice per month):**

First meeting (beginning of month): This meeting focuses on goal setting for the month and reviewing the successes and challenges from the previous month. It's a time for leaders to help staff members clarify their priorities and plan their work accordingly.

Second meeting (mid-month check-in): The mid-month check-in is a shorter meeting to review progress on monthly goals, offer support, and address any emerging challenges. It helps keep staff accountable for their goals while providing an opportunity to adjust plans if necessary.

Establishing this rhythm helps create consistency and predictability for the team, allowing everyone to understand when and where discussions will happen. This means fewer surprises and last-minute meetings, which can disrupt productivity. Additionally, having this regular cadence ensures that goals, priorities, and potential roadblocks are consistently addressed, preventing issues from being left unresolved for too long. It leads to greater accountability and people feel like communication flows smoothly.

Running Effective Meetings

Effective meetings are the backbone of a well-functioning parish. Meetings can often feel unproductive or unnecessarily long, but with proper structure, they become a tool for clear communication, accountability, and alignment. The goal is to ensure that everyone is present, updates are shared, commitments are reviewed, and the most pressing topics are discussed with clear outcomes.

Here's a framework for running effective leadership meetings that not only respects everyone's time but also drives results.

1. Segue: Helping Participants Become Present

Meetings should start by helping participants transition from their previous tasks or distractions and become fully present. This can be done with a short segue that allows people to focus and set the tone for the meeting. Examples include:

A moment of silence or prayer: Begin the meeting with a prayer or moment of silence to invite the Holy Spirit into the discussion. This helps ground the meeting in the parish's mission and spiritual goals.

A reflection or quote: Share a meaningful quote from Scripture or a saint to inspire focus and remind the team why their work matters.

A brief personal update: Allow each team member to share a short, positive personal or professional update. This helps to break the ice, build camaraderie, and make sure everyone feels engaged before diving into the agenda.

2. Updates: People and the Parish

After the segue, move on to **any updates about people on the team or in the parish**. This is important for maintaining connection and care within your community. Examples of updates to share include:

Team member updates: If someone on the team is dealing with a personal matter or has accomplished something significant, acknowledge it. For example, "John will be out next week due to a family matter" or "Sarah's event last weekend was a great success."

Parish updates: Share relevant information about the parish, such as new parishioners, significant events, or important feedback from the community. These updates keep everyone on the same page about what's happening in the broader parish community.

3. Review of Previous To-Do Items

Accountability is crucial to running effective meetings. Take a few moments to **review the to-do items that were committed to in the last meeting**. This step

ensures that there is follow-through on tasks and provides an opportunity for individuals to report on their progress.

Quick status updates: Each team member responsible for a task from the previous meeting should briefly report whether the task is complete, in progress, or if they've encountered obstacles.

Focus on accountability, not blame: The goal is to ensure that tasks move forward, not to criticize. If something hasn't been done, discuss what support is needed or what the next steps are. Name it; don't look for blame or shame.

4. Review of the Parish Scorecard

A **review of the parish scorecard** allows the team to assess how the parish is performing on key metrics. The scorecard should be a simple tool that tracks important data points such as Mass attendance, financial health, ministry participation, or progress toward specific goals.

Discuss metrics briefly: Focus on metrics that are off track or require discussion. If a certain area is falling behind, it may become a discussion item for this meeting or scheduled for future attention.

Celebrate wins: If there are metrics showing positive progress, take a moment to celebrate those successes.

5. Discussion Items: Structure for Productive Dialogue

Next, move to the **list of discussion items for this meeting**. Each discussion should have the following components to ensure focus and clarity:

Desired outcome: Start with the end in mind. What decision or outcome do you hope to achieve by the end of the discussion? This ensures that everyone knows what the goal is.

Background facts: Provide the facts relevant to the discussion. This could be data, feedback, or information gathered since the last meeting.

Assumptions: Highlight any assumptions that are guiding the discussion, so the team can address them if needed.

Discussion agenda: Lay out a few key points or questions that will guide the conversation. For example, if you're discussing a new outreach program, the agenda might include "Who will lead this effort?" and "What resources do we need?"

Each discussion item should be timed to keep the meeting on track, and it's important to designate someone to facilitate or guide the conversation so that it remains focused on achieving the desired outcome.

6. To-Do List: Action Steps Identified During the Meeting

After the discussion, compile a **list of to-do items that are identified during the meeting**. Each to-do item should follow the critical format of:

Next step: What is the exact task that needs to be completed?

Due date: When does this task need to be finished? Remember, tasks should be broken down into steps that can be completed within a week.

Responsible person: Who is responsible for completing the task? Clearly assigning ownership is essential for ensuring accountability.

This simple formula of **"Next Step, Due Date, and Responsible Party"** is one of the most powerful tools for effective management. It ensures that every decision made in the meeting translates into actionable tasks with clear accountability.

7. Communication: What Needs to Be Shared After the Meeting

Before closing, it's important to make a **list of what needs to be communicated to others outside the meeting**. This might include:

Updates to staff or volunteers: If decisions made in the meeting will impact other people, ensure that there is a plan to communicate the changes or updates clearly.

Parish-wide announcements: If there is something that needs to be shared with the entire parish, determine the best method of communication (e.g., through the bulletin, email, or pulpit announcements).

Assign responsibility for these communications to specific individuals so that nothing falls through the cracks.

By following this structure, you can ensure that your meetings are focused, productive, and lead to real outcomes.

Agenda Item	Time Range	Schedule Example
01. Prayer	1-2 mins	9:00 – 9:02
02. Opening Segue A short activity to help participants become present (good news, personal or professional, reflection, personal update)	2-5 mins	9:02 – 9:05
03. Team and Parish Updates Share any personal or professional updates about team members or parishioners	3-5 mins	9:05 – 9:10
04. Review of Previous To-Do Items Quick status updates on action items committed in the last meeting	2-5 mins	9:10 – 9:15
05. Review of Parish Scorecard Discuss key metrics, celebrate wins, identify areas needing attention	1-5 mins	9:15 – 9:20
06. Discussion Item 1 *First discussion topic:* Desired outcome, background facts, assumptions, and agenda (e.g., new outreach program)	5-20 mins	9:20 – 9:40
07. Discussion Item 2	5-20 mins	9:40 – 10:00
08. Discussion Item 3 (if needed)	3-15 mins	10:00 – 10:15
09. To-Do-List and Action Items *Identify new action items:* Next step, due date, and responsible person	4-10 mins	10:15 – 10:25
10. Communication Plan Decide what needs to be communicated outside the meeting and assign responsibility	2-5 mins	10:25 – 10:30

Applying the Meeting Framework to Other Parish Meetings

The structured approach to meetings outlined in the previous section can easily be adapted for various types of meetings throughout your parish, whether they involve volunteers, departmental teams, or 1:1s with staff and volunteers. Using a consistent meeting framework not only promotes clarity and efficiency but also fosters a culture of accountability and purpose across the parish. Let's look at how this structure can be applied to different meeting types.

Benefits of a Consistent Meeting Framework

By applying this structured meeting framework across various meeting types, you ensure that:

Consistency is maintained: No matter the setting—whether it's a volunteer meeting, a departmental meeting, or a 1:1—the format remains familiar and fosters accountability.

Clear outcomes are achieved: The framework ensures that each meeting ends with clear next steps, responsible individuals, and deadlines, making it easy to track progress.

Focus is maintained: Each section of the meeting is designed to move the conversation forward, preventing the meeting from going off-topic or becoming unproductive.

Spiritual focus is kept: By starting meetings with a spiritual segue, you remind everyone involved that their work serves a greater mission. This helps participants stay grounded in the purpose of the parish and their role within it.

This meeting structure can be adapted for any context within the parish, ensuring that meetings are purposeful, time-efficient, and aligned with the parish's mission. By maintaining a consistent approach across all types of meetings, you create a culture of clarity, accountability, and mission-driven progress.

The Daily Huddle

What Are Daily Huddles?

Daily huddles, sometimes referred to as **stand-ups**, are short, focused meetings that typically last no more than fifteen minutes. They're designed to quickly align the team on what was accomplished yesterday, what the focus is for today, and any obstacles or challenges that may be blocking progress. The goal of the huddle is to ensure the team is in sync, aware of each other's priorities, and able to address issues before they become larger problems. These meetings are intentionally brief, keeping the conversation focused and efficient.

Why Do We Call Them Huddles?

Just like sports teams huddle between plays to make sure everyone is on the same page, in a parish setting, a daily huddle is a quick check-in to ensure the team is aligned on priorities before they "get back on the field" for the day. They are sometimes called **stand-ups** because they are meant to be short and to the point, often with participants literally standing to keep the energy high and to avoid the meeting dragging on.

We don't run huddles on team meeting days, as those larger, more in-depth discussions should cover the day's needs, and there's no reason to duplicate effort.

How to Run an Effective Daily Huddle

Daily huddles should follow a consistent structure to maintain efficiency. The goal is to give everyone a quick status update, raise any concerns, and move forward. Here's how to run them:

1. **Keep it under fifteen minutes**: The huddle is designed to be a quick check-in, not a detailed discussion or problem-solving session. Timeboxing it to fifteen minutes ensures it stays on track. It doesn't have to be at the beginning of the day, especially if some key members have other schedules, such as the priests coming after daily mass.
2. **Three key topics**: Each participant shares updates on three key topics:

a. **What did you accomplish yesterday?** (top three completed items)

b. **What are you focusing on today?** (top three priorities for the day)

c. **Are you blocked by anything?** (Is there anything preventing you from moving forward?)

3. This simple format keeps the conversation focused on daily progress and helps the team spot any emerging issues before they become serious obstacles.

4. **No problem-solving during the huddle**: If someone mentions that they're blocked, acknowledge it and follow up after the huddle to address the problem. The huddle should move quickly, so it's not the time to deep dive into solutions.

5. **No huddles on team meeting day**: On days when a full team meeting is scheduled, there's no need for a daily huddle. The team meeting will already cover goals, progress, and issues in more detail, so the huddle is unnecessary.

The Parish Protocol: Navigating Preferences and Making Decisions

As your parish team grows, you'll inevitably encounter situations where staff members have differing experiences, preferences, or ways of doing things. While diversity of thought is valuable, it's also important to have **consistency** in how the parish operates. This is where the **Parish Protocol** comes in—deciding on a unified way of handling processes, tools, and decisions where there may not be a "right" or "wrong" but simply a **preferred method** that everyone follows for the sake of clarity and efficiency.

The Parish Protocol helps ensure that the entire parish operates in alignment, avoiding confusion, inefficiency, or duplicated effort. While there's flexibility in certain areas, it's important that the parish team agrees on and adheres to shared standards that support smooth collaboration and consistent results.

Below are some common examples of decisions your parish may face when defining the Parish Protocol (keep in mind there are many other good options, not just the two we present here):

Technology Platforms (Google Docs vs. Microsoft Word)

One of the most common points of divergence in many organizations is around the use of technology. For example, using Google Workspace or Microsoft Office. This debate can be as heated as any political or religious debate.

Your parish will need to decide on a consistent platform to avoid confusion, document version control issues, and collaboration challenges. Choosing one tool as part of the Parish Protocol ensures everyone is working from the same system and improves efficiency.

Project Management Tools

When managing parish projects, having everyone use the same project management tool can greatly enhance collaboration and tracking.

Once your team grows, it's helpful to settle on one platform as the standard. This prevents confusion and ensures that all projects are being managed in the same way, creating consistency in workflows.

Ministry Planning Tools

For ministries like music, events, or volunteer coordination, there are different planning tools available.

Deciding on one platform helps ministries run smoothly and ensures that volunteers and staff know where to go for scheduling, planning, and communication.

Social Media Management

Managing the parish's social media presence across platforms can become confusing if different staff members prefer different tools.

By settling on one tool for social media management, your parish communications can be streamlined, ensuring consistent messaging across all platforms.

Accounting Systems

The choice of accounting software is critical for maintaining financial transparency and efficiency.

Choosing one accounting system as part of the Parish Protocol helps streamline financial processes and ensures accurate, consistent reporting. Sometimes this will be mandated by the diocese.

Online Giving Platforms

Online giving has become an important part of parish operations. Some staff may have preferences for different platforms.

Selecting a single platform as the parish standard simplifies the giving process for parishioners and staff alike, avoiding confusion and streamlining financial operations.

Alignment Across the Diocese

At some point, it may make sense for **alignment across entire dioceses** to take place, particularly when parishes are working together or sharing resources. This broader alignment can improve collaboration across parish communities, simplify training, and ensure consistency in how tools are used across the diocese. It also allows for centralized support and troubleshooting, which can be especially helpful when managing technology platforms or processes.

For parishes looking for guidance, we've provided a **workbook** with examples of frameworks and tools being used by other parishes, which can be easily adopted. These frameworks are designed to help you make decisions that create consistency within your parish, and they offer best practices from other communities that have successfully implemented their own Parish Protocols.

While there's no single "right" answer when choosing your Parish Protocol, the key is to ensure **alignment**.

Aligning the Organization

Creating alignment within a parish is a gradual, thoughtful process that builds on the foundational work we've discussed throughout this book. Without a clear sense of identity, mission, and operational structure, achieving alignment becomes nearly impossible. So, if you haven't already, take time to revisit earlier concepts to ensure you're building on solid ground.

Alignment in a parish is about ensuring that all groups—staff, volunteers, ministries, and councils—are working harmoniously toward the same goals. Each part of the parish must not only understand the parish's mission but be able to articulate how their specific role contributes to that mission. This isn't just about agreeing on a direction; it's about operationalizing that direction in a way that is practical, measurable, and consistent across the organization.

Before we get into the practical steps, keep in mind all that we talked about in Chapter 5, Meeting People Where They Are. Many people in the parish, even very committed volunteers, because of where they are on their faith journey, might not understand why the leadership team wants to make certain things a priority. Sometimes, taking these practical steps helps foster the deeper conversation of why there are conflicts and how to overcome them through the lens of the mission of the Church as well as our personal stories of faith and conversion.

One tool that can greatly help in fostering alignment is the creation of a **two-page plan** for each group or department. This two-page plan helps to crystallize the group's specific mission, goals, and processes while ensuring that their work is in sync with the overall parish strategy.

Practical Steps to Foster Alignment

Get to know the groups and their leaders: Start by building relationships with the leaders of each ministry and group in your parish. This process is not just about formal meetings but about genuine connection. Spend time attending their events, sharing meals, and having informal conversations. These interactions will help you understand their perspectives, motivations, and challenges.

Listen to their history and understand their motivations: Every group in the parish has a unique history and set of motivations. Take time to listen to where they've come from, their goals, and what drives them to serve. This will help you guide them toward alignment while respecting their origins and purpose.

Invite them to formation sessions: Regular formation sessions are a powerful tool for alignment. These sessions allow for spiritual formation, coordination around the parish's mission and values, and practical discussions around logistics like room scheduling or event planning. Through prayer and formation, you can foster both spiritual and operational unity.

Develop a Two-Page Plan for Each Group: To ensure alignment, each group within the parish should have a two-page plan that outlines their mission, goals, and strategies. This plan includes:

- **Mission statement**: a clear, concise description of the group's purpose within the parish and how it aligns with the overall mission
- **Quarterly and annual goals**: specific, measurable objectives that help track progress
- **Key processes**: core activities that the group will focus on to achieve these goals
- **Metrics for success**: how the group will measure whether they are on or off plan, which might include participation numbers, engagement levels, or financial benchmarks
- **Budget requirements**: a detailed outline of the financial resources needed to meet the group's goals, including funds for materials, events, and any ongoing operational costs
- **Staffing and volunteer requirements**: a clear description of the people needed, including specific roles for staff and volunteers, the number of hours required, and any necessary training or recruitment efforts to support the group's activities and objectives

This plan not only provides clarity but also ensures that each group is strategically aligned with the broader goals of the parish. It serves as a living document that leaders can reference and adjust as the parish's needs evolve.

You can find an example of this plan in the accompanying workbook

1. **Assess alignment and adjust commitment:** Once you understand each group's purpose and plan, assess how well they align with the parish's mission. This assessment helps you determine how much support or resources to allocate to each group. Alignment is a two-way street—groups that closely align with the parish's mission should be given more support, while those that are less aligned may need to re-evaluate their direction or contribution.

2. **Offer pathways for growth:** After assessing alignment, offer groups and individuals clear pathways for growth, both spiritually and in terms of their ministry work. Encourage them to take steps forward in their formation and stewardship, always tying their progress back to the parish's larger mission.

3. **Hold regular meetings with clear agendas:** Regular, structured meetings are crucial to maintaining alignment. Each meeting should include:

   a. A review of progress toward goals

   b. Clear assignments and follow-ups on tasks

   c. Time for addressing challenges and celebrating successes

   d. Discussion on how each group's work is contributing to the parish's mission

4. **Evaluate and realign regularly:** Alignment requires ongoing review and adjustment. Regular check-ins, using the two-page plans, will help you track progress, identify areas of misalignment, and make necessary adjustments. These meetings provide opportunities for continuous improvement and allow each group to remain focused on their role in advancing the parish's mission.

Linking Long-Term Goals to Quarterly and Daily Work

Your parish's long-term success is driven by the consistent, focused actions taken on a quarterly and daily basis. Once long-term goals are set, it's important to break them down into smaller, actionable objectives. This is where the two-page plan comes in. Each quarter, review progress toward these smaller objectives, ensuring that day-to-day efforts contribute to the larger mission.

For example, if your long-term goal is to increase parish engagement, your quarterly objectives might include:

- ⏩ Launching a new ministry by the end of the first quarter
- ⏩ Improving outreach to young families through targeted events
- ⏩ Increasing volunteer participation by 10% within six months

The meeting rhythm described above helps to ensure that these goals are then scaled down to the monthly, weekly, and daily levels to actually get them done.

In the words of Saint Paul,

> *"For just as the body is one and has many members, and all the members of the body, though many, are one body, so it is with Christ."*
>
> **1 CORINTHIANS 12:12**

This biblical wisdom reminds us that while we have many different groups and individuals within our parish, we are all part of one body in Christ. Alignment is about helping each part recognize its role in the whole and work in harmony with the others.

11

CHAPTER

Putting It All Together

Now that we've explored the key concepts for managing your parish, it's time to turn our attention to how these ideas come to life in practice. Effective leadership doesn't just stop at understanding values, setting goals, or aligning teams; it requires ongoing reflection, deliberate action, and continual growth. This chapter will guide you through a practical process for assessing where your parish stands today, implementing the strategies discussed throughout this book, and fostering an environment of continuous administrative growth in service of the mission.

Let's dive into the steps that will help you turn the vision of this book into reality for your parish.

How to Assess Your Current Position as a Parish

Before you can move forward with new strategies or initiatives, it's critical to first assess where your parish currently stands. A thorough assessment provides clarity on your strengths, challenges, and areas for growth, allowing you to develop a focused plan for the future. This isn't just about the operations of the parish but also how well you're living out your mission and serving the spiritual needs of your community. This might feel overwhelming if you're afraid of critical feedback, so it is important to look for the truth and not take negative feedback about the parish's weaknesses as a personal attack or criticism. Naming the truth does not assign blame but rather helps find the problems. Also keep in mind that often people know where problems are but aren't well equipped to know how to solve them.

One of the best tools for this assessment is creating a **two-page plan** for the parish, similar to the plans we discussed for individual groups in chapter 10. This plan provides a concise overview of your parish's mission, goals, processes, and resources, giving you a clear picture of your current state and areas for improvement.

1. Mission and Vision Alignment

The first step in your assessment is to evaluate how well your parish's current activities align with its mission and vision. Your mission is the guiding purpose of your parish, and everything you do should flow from it.

To assess this:

Review your parish's mission and vision statements. Do we know what they are? Are they still relevant? Do they clearly communicate the purpose of your parish, and do they inspire action among your staff, volunteers, and parishioners?

Evaluate your ministries and activities. Do they support your mission, or have some become disconnected from it over time? If a ministry or event doesn't contribute to fulfilling your mission, it may need to be reevaluated or refocused.

Include this in your two-page plan:

>> **Mission statement**: Clearly define your parish's mission and vision in the first section of your two-page plan.

2. Assessing Ministries and Programs

Once you've revisited your mission, it's time to take a closer look at the effectiveness of your ministries and programs. This is not just about participation numbers but also about the spiritual fruit that these activities produce.

Consider the following:

>> Which ministries are thriving, and which are struggling? Are there programs that are no longer meeting the needs of your community?
>> How do your ministries contribute to evangelization, discipleship, and the overall mission of the Church?
>> Are your ministry leaders well-supported, and do they have clear direction?

Include this in your two-page plan:

Key processes: List the core activities and ministries your parish is engaged in and assess whether they are effectively contributing to the parish's goals.

3. Financial and Resource Assessment

A parish's ability to fulfill its mission is closely tied to how it stewards its resources. This includes not only financial health but also how well you are managing people— staff and volunteers.

To assess this:

▸▸ **Review your budget.** Are you using parish funds effectively to support key ministries and operational needs? Are there areas where resources are being stretched too thin or underutilized?

▸▸ **Assess your facilities and physical resources.** Are they adequate to support current ministries and future growth?

Take stock of your staffing and volunteers. Do you have the right people in the right roles? Are you managing volunteer resources effectively to meet the parish's needs?

Include this in your two-page plan:

▸▸ **Budget requirements**: Outline the financial resources needed for your key ministries and activities.

▸▸ **Staffing and volunteer requirements**: Clearly define the people resources—staff and volunteers—necessary to support the work of the parish.

4. Measuring Success and Accountability

Lastly, evaluate how well you are tracking progress and measuring success. This is critical for knowing whether your parish is on or off track.

To assess this:

What metrics are you currently using to measure the health of the parish? This could include Mass attendance, sacramental participation, ministry engagement, or financial benchmarks.

Do you have regular review processes in place to evaluate whether you are moving toward your goals? Are there accountability structures that help ensure progress is made?

Include this in your two-page plan:

Metrics for success: Identify the key metrics that will help you track progress toward your parish's mission and goals.

By using this two-page plan as your assessment tool, you can gain a clear understanding of where your parish currently stands and create a focused plan for moving forward. This assessment provides the foundation for implementing the concepts in this book and ensuring your parish remains aligned with its mission.

How to Introduce the Concepts in This Book to Your Parish Team

Introducing new concepts to your parish team can be a delicate process, especially when these ideas require changes to how the parish operates. It's not uncommon to face resistance from staff or volunteers who have varying business experiences and are comfortable with familiar ways of doing things. However, with a clear plan, thoughtful communication, and a willingness to listen to concerns, you can successfully introduce the principles in this book to your parish team. Keep in mind that while some resistance is normal, too much resistance might show that they are the wrong people to have on the team.

Here's how to approach this process:

1. Have Them Read This Book—Start with Key Sections

It's important that your staff and key volunteer leaders understand the principles and frameworks outlined in this book. While expecting them to read the entire book upfront may be overwhelming, you can break it down into manageable steps:

Assign key sections to read first: Start with the most critical sections that apply to your parish's immediate needs, such as those on mission, strategy, and team alignment. Encourage each team member to focus on these initial chapters.

Set deadlines: Give your team a reasonable deadline for reading the assigned sections. Allow time for reflection and note-taking so they come prepared to discuss their insights.

Hold a group discussion: Once the key sections have been read, gather your team for an open discussion. Ask questions like *What stood out to you?* or *How do you see this aligning with our parish's current needs?* This will help everyone start thinking about how to apply these concepts to your specific context.

2. Prepare Your Team for Year 1

Once your team is familiar with the basic concepts, it's time to prepare them for the first year of implementation. Yes, this does imply this is a multi-year process, and we've seen that holds true consistently. This is where you start translating the book's ideas into action. Here's how to do that effectively.

Outline the year's goals: Start by explaining the long-term vision and goals for the first year. Be clear about how the concepts in the book will help the parish achieve its mission, improve processes, and build a stronger community.

Provide a high-level roadmap: Walk through the high-level steps for Year 1 implementation (as discussed in the previous section). Explain the key milestones for each quarter, such as the development of two-page plans, quarterly evaluations, and adjustments.

Emphasize the importance of teamwork: Make it clear that this process will require cooperation and collaboration across all ministries and departments. The team needs to understand that success will come from everyone working together, not in silos. Use a team building approach, potentially with an assessment to discuss how you work together.

3. Handle Objections Effectively

You should anticipate objections from staff and key volunteers, particularly those with strong business backgrounds or long-standing habits. These objections might include:

▸ *"We've always done it this way, and it works."*

▸ *"This approach doesn't align with my business experience."*

▸ *"Why should we change when things are already running smoothly?"*

Here's how to address these concerns head-on:

Acknowledge their expertise and experience: It's important to validate the knowledge and skills that each team member brings to the table. Acknowledge that their business experience is valuable but explain that the parish operates differently than a corporation. The goal is not to impose rigid business practices but to use helpful management tools that allow for flexibility and growth within the unique spiritual and operational needs of the parish.

Show how these concepts serve the parish's mission: Make sure to frame every new concept or strategy in terms of how it serves the mission of the Church. Highlight that the primary goal of this book is not just operational efficiency but a stronger alignment with the parish's mission of evangelization, community building, and discipleship. Remind your team that these tools are meant to serve people and the mission, not the other way around.

Share success stories from other parishes: One effective way to handle objections is by sharing real-life examples of other parishes that have successfully implemented these concepts. If possible, use testimonials or case studies from parishes that have worked with John Oberg Advisory or adopted similar frameworks. This can help reassure skeptical team members that these changes are achievable and beneficial.

Invite participation, not just compliance: People are more likely to embrace change when they feel heard and involved in the process. Invite team members to provide their input and ideas on how best to implement the concepts in the book. This collaborative approach will help them feel more ownership over the process and reduce resistance.

Address the "comfort zone" issue directly: Some staff and volunteers may prefer to continue doing things the way they always have because it's comfortable. Be clear that growth and mission-driven progress often require stepping out of comfort zones. Reiterate that you're not abandoning what works but building on it with proven strategies that will allow the parish to flourish in new ways. You might say, "We're not here to change everything; we're here to strengthen and align what's already in place." Most people can buy into new ideas when they feel they've been part of the process, but some might decide to leave, and that's an acceptable outcome.

4. Follow Up Regularly

Implementation isn't a "set it and forget it" process—it requires consistent follow-up and accountability. Here's how to keep the momentum going:

Hold regular check-ins: Schedule regular meetings (weekly or biweekly) with your leadership team to discuss progress and any challenges they're facing. Use these sessions to revisit concepts from the book and ensure everyone is staying aligned with the implementation plan.

Track progress against the two-page plans: As each ministry develops and executes its two-page plan, track their progress using the metrics and goals they've outlined. Celebrate wins and address roadblocks as they arise.

Be patient but persistent: Implementing new ideas takes time. Be patient with your team but also persistent in keeping everyone accountable to the overall plan. Remind them regularly that the work they're doing is essential for the long-term success of the parish.

5. Celebrate Progress

Finally, don't forget to celebrate the progress your team makes along the way. Recognize both big milestones (such as completing key initiatives) and small wins (like improved communication or a successful ministry event). Celebrating success helps build momentum and reinforces the positive impact of these changes.

By approaching the introduction of these concepts with a clear plan, open communication, and respect for your team's input, you can create a collaborative environment where everyone is invested in the parish's mission and excited to move forward together.

How to Implement the Topics in This Book

Once you've assessed your parish's current position, the next step is to begin the implementation of the strategies and principles outlined in this book. Implementation is a process that requires careful planning, clear communication, and consistent follow-through. In this section, we will provide an implementation framework that begins with an assessment and continues through a structured plan for Year 1.

1. Conduct a 20-Question Assessment for Staff and Key Volunteers

The first practical step in your implementation journey is to engage your staff and key volunteers in a 20-question assessment which you can find in the workbook. This assessment will help gauge where your leadership team currently stands in terms of understanding and aligning with the key concepts presented in this book. You can discuss the results with your team, understanding better where they are at and what the obstacles might be moving forward. That will create more buy-in for these concepts and their implementation. It will also serve as a benchmark for tracking progress over time. You can find it in the workbook.

2. Key Steps for Implementation: A Year 1 Plan

Now that you have gathered baseline data from the assessment, it's time to develop a structured plan for implementation. Successful implementation should be phased over time, beginning with a clear kickoff and focusing on specific goals for the first year.

One-Day Kickoff Event

A well-planned one-day kickoff event is essential for launching your implementation journey. This event will bring together your leadership team, key volunteers, and staff to communicate the vision and strategy behind the implementation process.

What to cover at the kickoff event:

- **Opening prayer and spiritual reflection**: Center the day on the mission of the parish and Christ's calling.

➡ **Presentation of the assessment results**: Review the findings from the 20-question assessment to ensure transparency and highlight areas for improvement.

➡ **Overview of the plan**: Present the high-level goals for the year, broken down by quarter, and explain how these align with the parish's mission.

➡ **Two-page plans**: Introduce or review the two-page plans for each ministry or department, ensuring everyone understands their role in the implementation.

➡ **Commitments and next steps**: Have each leader commit to specific actions they will take over the next quarter and establish regular check-ins for accountability.

High-Level Steps for Year 1
Q1: Solidify Leadership and Begin Strategic Alignment

➡ **Define leadership roles**: Ensure that your leadership team and key volunteers have clearly defined roles and responsibilities aligned with the mission.

➡ **Develop two-page plans**: Have each ministry or group develop their two-page plan, including mission statement, key processes, goals, metrics for success, budget requirements, and staffing needs.

➡ **Communicate the plan**: Ensure that the entire parish staff understands the goals and objectives for the year and their individual role in achieving them.

Q2: Begin Implementation of Key Priorities

➡ **Focus on top priorities:** Identify the most pressing issues revealed by your assessment and begin implementing solutions. This might include improving communication, reorganizing ministries, or addressing financial concerns. Less is more when it comes to picking priorities, so if you can identify the one most important thing and focus on that, then you can work on other things later.

➡ **Establish accountability**: Set up regular check-in meetings for leaders and ministry heads to report on progress toward their goals.

➡ **Build momentum**: Begin to implement the action steps outlined in each two-page plan, ensuring alignment with the overall parish mission.

Q3: Evaluate Progress and Make Adjustments

▸ **Mid-year review**: Conduct a mid-year review of all ministries and programs to assess progress toward goals. Use the metrics from the two-page plans to determine if you are on or off track.

▸ **Address roadblocks**: Identify any obstacles that have arisen and adjust strategies as necessary. This could mean reallocating resources, revising goals, or changing leadership roles where needed.

▸ **Reengage the team**: Use this review to reengage staff and volunteers, offering further training or resources where necessary to keep momentum going.

Q4: Plan for Next Year and Deepen Engagement

▸ **End-of-year evaluation**: Conduct a full evaluation of the implementation process. What worked? What didn't? Use this reflection to plan for the upcoming year.

▸ **Deepen parish engagement**: As alignment begins to take hold, focus on deepening engagement with the broader parish community. Introduce new initiatives or ministries that reflect the parish's evolving needs.

▸ **Celebrate success**: Celebrate the successes of Year 1, recognizing the efforts of staff and volunteers who contributed to the progress.

With this structured approach, you can effectively implement the concepts from this book, building on your parish's strengths and addressing its challenges in a clear, phased process. The Year 1 plan lays the foundation for continued growth and alignment, ensuring that your parish remains mission-focused and sustainable over the long term.

How to Continue Your Administrative Growth for Mission

Management in a parish setting is not just about efficiency or processes—it's an essential part of your pastoral journey and a reflection of your role as a shepherd. Just as a shepherd cares for the well-being of their flock, pastors must manage the resources, people, and ministries entrusted to them to fulfill the mission of the Church. Understanding and developing these administrative skills is an ongoing process that requires intention, balance, and deep reliance on your own relationship with Christ.

1. Embrace Management as Part of Your Pastoral Calling

Managing a parish is not separate from your pastoral duties; it's integral to your vocation as a leader. The skills of management—strategic planning, resource allocation, team leadership—are spiritual in nature because they serve the Church's mission of evangelization, community-building, and discipleship.

We've discussed various strategies and tools that can help you organize your parish more effectively. Mastering these skills is not a one-time effort. Just like pastoral care, administration is something you grow into and refine over time. Your role as a pastor requires spiritual and administrative development if you are to teach, sanctify, and govern the people of God entrusted to you.

2. Practice Balance: Pastoral, Administrative, and Self-Care

One of the most important aspects of your leadership is maintaining balance. This book has emphasized the need to balance pastoral and administrative responsibilities, but as a pastor, it's also crucial to balance those demands with self-care.

Running a parish can be overwhelming, and it's easy to become consumed by the day-to-day management tasks. But neglecting your own well-being—whether spiritual, emotional, or physical—will inevitably impact your ability to serve. Self-care is not a luxury; it's a necessity for sustaining your energy and effectiveness as a leader. You have heard these things in the seminary, but now you're in the real world of the parish, so ask yourself, "Will my bishop ever encourage me to work so hard I burn out?" The answer is of course "no", he wants you to have a healthy and thriving priesthood that lasts for many years to come.

Practical steps for balance:

Set boundaries: Create clear boundaries between work and personal time. Ensure that you have moments of rest, reflection, and recreation, just as you encourage your parishioners to do. You might have periods of intense work, but that cannot last long.

Delegate appropriately: Don't feel like you have to do everything yourself. Trust your staff and volunteers to take on key responsibilities so you can focus on the areas where you are most needed. Deacons were raised up by the apostles to assist with the administration of the Church's goods, and more and more parishes are asking them to assist with administration today. Just ensure they are working from the right framework.

Schedule time for prayer and spiritual renewal: As you manage the parish, don't neglect your own spiritual growth. Make time for personal prayer, retreats, and spiritual direction to stay connected to Christ and to recharge. These should be put at the best time of the day for you and to avoid interruptions.

When you are caring for your own needs, you are better equipped to care for the needs of your parish. Balance is key to longevity in leadership.

3. Share Your Personal Experience with Jesus

As a pastor, one of the most powerful tools you have is your personal experience with Jesus Christ. The leadership you provide to your parish is not just administrative; it's deeply spiritual, rooted in your own relationship with the Trinity. Sharing this personal experience with your staff and parishioners can inspire and guide them in their own faith journeys, so learn how to share your story, not only of your vocation but of your relationship with the Lord before and after ordination.

Why sharing your experience matters:

Authenticity breeds trust: When you openly share your relationship with Jesus, it helps people see you not just as a leader but as a fellow disciple walking the path of faith. This authenticity fosters trust and encourages others to be open about their own spiritual experiences.

Spiritual leadership starts from within: Your ability to lead others toward Christ is directly connected to your own ongoing relationship with Him. By sharing how you've experienced God's grace, love, and challenges in your own life, you create a bridge between your personal journey and your pastoral mission.

It strengthens your connection to the Trinity: Regularly reflecting on and sharing with others your personal relationship with the Father, Son, and Holy Spirit helps deepen that connection to God through healthy attachment, which in turn strengthens your pastoral leadership.

Incorporate moments in your leadership—whether in meetings, homilies, or one-on-one conversations—where you can share how your personal relationship with Jesus informs your ministry. This can be as simple as offering a reflection on how prayer has guided a decision or how a challenge has strengthened your trust in God.

4. Commit to Lifelong Learning

Just as your spiritual growth is an ongoing process, so is your development as a leader and administrator. Effective management requires not only refining the skills you've learned but also staying open to new ideas and opportunities for growth.

Lifelong learning in administrative leadership involves:

Ongoing education: Consider attending workshops, conferences, or retreats focused on parish management, leadership, or pastoral care. Many dioceses offer resources for pastors to continue their learning, and organizations like John Oberg Advisory provide specialized guidance in these areas.

Mentorship and peer support: Build relationships with other pastors who are also focused on administrative growth. Mentorship and peer discussions can offer valuable insights and encouragement as you navigate the challenges of leadership.

Regular reflection: Set aside time each quarter or year to reflect on your growth as a pastor and an administrator. What have you learned? Where do you need more development? This habit of self-reflection will help ensure that you are continually improving in your role.

5. Celebrate Milestones and Progress

As you grow in your administrative capabilities, it's important to recognize and celebrate the progress made, personally and as a parish. Celebrating milestones doesn't just motivate you—it builds a culture of gratitude and positivity within the parish.

Celebrate when:

- ⏩ A key ministry goal is achieved.
- ⏩ Your parish makes strides in aligning with its mission.
- ⏩ Personal growth or breakthroughs occur, whether in spiritual leadership or administrative efficiency.

These celebrations help sustain the energy and momentum needed for long-term success in your parish leadership journey.

Conclusion: Stepping Boldly into Your Mission

As you reach the end of this book, it's important to pause and reflect on the journey you've taken. You've explored the fundamental elements of leading a parish—aligning mission, building teams, managing resources, solving problems, and ensuring that all of your efforts serve the greater purpose of spreading the Gospel. But more than that, you've come to see how **management** and **mission** are not separate responsibilities but intertwined aspects of your pastoral calling.

Leadership in the Church is a sacred task. It's about shepherding people toward Christ, and effective management is one of the ways you can do that more faithfully. You now have the tools to guide your parish with clarity, purpose, and grace—always striving to keep Christ at the center of everything you do.

Trust that God will give you the strength, insight, and perseverance you need to shepherd your parish. Step boldly into your role, knowing that your work will bear fruit for the Kingdom, and that every small victory is a testament to the glory of God.

You are ready to lead, ready to inspire, ready to make an impact for Christ. May God bless you in every step of this journey and may your parish thrive under your faithful and compassionate leadership.

"I can do all things through Him who strengthens me."

PHILIPPIANS 4:13

www.ingramcontent.com/pod-product-compliance
Lightning Source LLC
Chambersburg PA
CBHW060505130626
46553CB00002B/412

* 9 7 9 8 9 9 0 9 5 8 0 4 3 *